DETROIT PUBLIC LIBRARY
3 5674 00330
W9-CIH-700

# TOYS IN THE ATTIC

A new play by LILLIAN HELLMAN

# TOYS IN THE ATTIC

Random House, New York

 Published in New York by Random House, Inc., and simultaneously in Toronto, Canada, by Random House of Canada, Limited.



Photographs by courtesy of Cantor-Secunda

Library of Congress Catalog Card Number: 60–12144

Manufactured in the United States of America

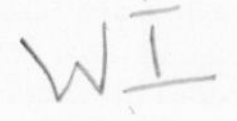

*For*
*RICHARD WILBUR*

TOYS IN THE ATTIC *was first presented by Kermit Bloomgarden at the Hudson Theatre, New York City, on February 25, 1960, with the following cast:*

(IN ORDER OF APPEARANCE)

| | |
|---|---|
| CARRIE BERNIERS | Maureen Stapleton |
| ANNA BERNIERS | Anne Revere |
| GUS | Charles McRae |
| ALBERTINE PRINE | Irene Worth |
| HENRY SIMPSON | Percy Rodriguez |
| JULIAN BERNIERS | Jason Robards, Jr. |
| LILY BERNIERS | Rochelle Oliver |
| TAXI DRIVER | William Hawley |
| THREE MOVING MEN | Clifford Cothren, Tom Manley, Maurice Ellis |

*Directed by* Arthur Penn

*Setting and lighting by* Howard Bay

*Costumes by* Ruth Morley

PLACE: The Berniers house in New Orleans.

ACT ONE

SIX P.M. on a summer day.

ACT TWO

EIGHT A.M. the following morning.

ACT THREE

Shortly after.

# ACT ONE

# ACT ONE

*Place: The* Berniers' *living room, the entrance porch to the house, and a small city garden off the porch. The house is solid middle-class of another generation. The furniture is heavy and old. Everything inside and outside is neat, but in need of repairs. The porch has two rocking chairs and is crowded with plants. The garden has a table and chairs that have been painted too often and don't stay together very well. It is a house lived in by poor, clean, orderly people who don't like where they live.*

*At rise:* ANNA BERNIERS, *carrying her gloves and purse and still wearing her hat, pushes open the blinds of the windows that give on the garden. She lifts a large camellia pot and puts it outside. She pours a glass of water on the plant and moves back into the room to take off her hat.* ANNA *is a nice-looking woman, calm and quiet. She is about forty-two.* CARRIE BERNIERS *appears from the street, climbs the porch steps, and sits down in a porch chair. She is about thirty-eight, still pretty, but the prettiness is wearing thin and tired. She fans herself, rocks back and forth, the chair creaks and sways, and, wearily, she rises and moves to the other chair.*

CARRIE (*As she hears* ANNA *moving about in the kitchen*) That you, Anna?

ANNA (*Her voice*) Just got home.

CARRIE Hot.

ANNA Paper says a storm.

CARRIE I know. I'll take the plants in.

ANNA I just put them out. Let them have a little storm air.

CARRIE I don't like them out in a storm. Worries me. I don't like storms. I don't believe plants do, either.

ANNA (*Appears in the living room with a broom and a dust rag; speaks out toward the porch*) Did you have a hard day?

CARRIE He let me leave the office after lunch. "You're looking a little peaked, Miss Berniers, from the heat." I said I've been looking a little peaked for years in heat, in cold, in rain, when I was young, and now. You mean *you're* hot and want to go home, you faker, I said. Only I said it to myself.

ANNA We had a private sale at the store. Coats. Coats on a day like this. There was a very good bargain, red with black braid. I had my eye on it for you all last winter. But—

CARRIE Oh, I don't need a coat.

ANNA Yes, you do. Did you go to the park? I wanted to, but the sale went so late. Old lady Senlis and old lady Condelet just sat there, looking at everything, even small coats. How can rich people go to a sale on a day like this?

CARRIE I feel sorry for them. For all old ladies. Even rich ones. Money makes them lonely.

ANNA (*Laughs*) Why would that be?

CARRIE Don't you feel sorry for old ladies? You used to.

ANNA When my feet don't hurt and I don't have to sell them coats at a sale. Was it nice in the park?

CARRIE I didn't go to the park. I went to the cemetery.

ANNA (*Stops dusting, sighs*) Everybody still there?

CARRIE I took flowers. It's cool there. Cooler. I was the only person there. Nobody goes to see anybody in summer. Yet those who have passed away must be just as lonely in summer as they are in winter. Sometimes I think we shouldn't have put Mama and Papa at Mount Olive cemetery. Maybe it would have been nicer for them at Mount Great Hope with the new, rich people. What would you think if we don't get buried at Mount Olive with Mama and Papa?

ANNA Any place that's cool.

CARRIE I bought you a small bottle of Eau d'haut Alpine. Cologne water of the high Alps, I guess. (*Holds up a package*) Your weekly present. What did you buy me, may I ask, who shouldn't?

ANNA Jar of candied oranges.

CARRIE Oh, how nice. We'll have them for a savory. Do you know I read in our travel book on England that *they* think a proper savory is an anchovy. Anchovy after dinner. They won't make me eat it. What are you doing?

ANNA Nothing. I'm going to clean.

CARRIE Oh, don't. Sunday's cleaning day. Was this house always so big?

ANNA It grew as people left it.

CARRIE I want to tell you something I've never told you before. I never, ever, liked this house. Not even when we were children. I know *you* did, but I didn't.

ANNA You know I liked it?

CARRIE I don't think Julian ever liked it, either. That's why we used to have our supper out here on the steps. Did you ever know that's why I used to bring Julian out here, even when he was a baby, and we'd have our supper on the steps? I didn't want him to find out about the house. Julian and I. Nice of Mama and Papa to let us, wasn't it? Must have been a great deal of trouble carrying the dishes out here. Mama had an agreeable nature.

ANNA I carried the dishes out.

CARRIE Did you? Yes, so you did. Thank you, Anna. Thank you very much. Did you mind eating with Mama and Papa—(*Points off*)—in that awful oak tomb?

ANNA Yes, I minded.

CARRIE Well, it sure was a nice thing to do. I never knew you minded. Funny how you can live so close and long and not know things, isn't it?

ANNA Yes, indeed. I called Mr. Shine today. He said he hadn't had an inquiry in months. He said we should reduce the price of the house. I said we would, but there wasn't anything to reduce it to.

CARRIE (*Gets up, goes into the living room*) Oh, somebody'll come along will like it, you'll see.

ANNA Nobody's ever liked this house, nobody's ever going to.

CARRIE You always get mean to the house when something worries you. What's the matter?

ANNA And you always go to the cemetery.

CARRIE (*Opens the waist of her dress*) Just cooler. I so much like the French on the graves. *Un homme brave, mort pour la cité pendant la guerre*— Sounds better in French. A man gallant is so much more than just a gallant man. Nobody in our family's ever been killed in a war. Not Grandpapa, not Papa— Why, don't you think?

ANNA Some people get killed, some people don't.

CARRIE (*Laughs*) Papa always said he was scared to death and ran whenever he could. But Papa said just anything. Julian didn't like it when he said things like that. No little boy would. Papa shouldn't have talked that way.

ANNA Papa's been dead twenty-two years, Carrie. You should have taken it up with him before this.

CARRIE No letter for two weeks. I went to the main post office today, and said I was sure there'd been some confusion. Would they please call the other Berniers and see if a letter was there. And Alfie said, "Carrie, there are no other Berniers in New Orleans. There are some live in Biloxi, Mississippi, with a hardware store, but the central government of the United States does not give money to Louisiana to make calls to Mississippi, although maybe you could change that if you said it was Julian who had written the letter he didn't write." I was angry, but I didn't show it. How do you know it's Julian I am talking about, I said. We're expecting letters from Paris and Rome in reply to inquiries about our forthcoming tour.

(*She stops suddenly, run down*)

ANNA Julian's busy. That's all.

(GUS, *a colored man of about thirty-five, carrying a block of ice, comes up the porch steps*)

GUS You home?

ANNA We're home.

(GUS *goes off toward the kitchen*)

CARRIE (*Goes toward the piano*) I bought a book called *French Lessons in Songs*. I don't believe it. Never been two weeks before in his whole life. (*Softly, slowly*) I telephoned to Chicago and the hotel manager said Julian and Lily had moved months ago. Why didn't Julian tell us that?

ANNA (*Quietly*) I knew. I knew last week. Two letters came back here with address unknown. Carrie, Julian's married, he's moved away, he's got a business to take care of, he's busy. That's all.

CARRIE He's never been too busy to write or phone to us. You know that.

ANNA I know things have changed. That's as it should be.

CARRIE Yes, of course. Yes.

GUS (*Puts his head into the room*) Icebox all on one side. Miss Anna, you all sure need a new icebox. You all ought to treat yourselves.

ANNA You know, Gus, colored people are getting to talk just like white people. Kind of a shame.

GUS Ought to treat yourselves. Get a new little house, new little icebox. No more Julian to worry about. Just yourselves now to treat good.

CARRIE It's true. You getting to talk just like that white trash in my office. Just yourselves now and all that. (*With force*) Well, what do you think? We *are* going to treat ourselves good. We're going to sell this house and never come back. We're going on a great, big, long trip. For a *year,* or five. What do you think of that?

GUS (*To* ANNA) Ought to get yourselves a nice cat. I'll water the yard for you. Where are you going this time?

CARRIE Where we were always going. To Europe.

GUS You told me that last year. And I stopped the ice. And you told me around seven years back when Julian went on his other business trip, and I stopped the ice then—(*He laughs*) When I stop it now?

CARRIE (*Angry, too upset*) Very soon. *Very* soon. You hear me, Gus? *Very* soon. And if you just don't believe me you come around to church Sunday and hear us take a solemn oath right in church. We don't break a solemn oath in church.

GUS That's good. Lot of people do.

CARRIE How dare you, Gus? When I say a solemn oath in church?

ANNA (*To* GUS) There's food in the icebox. Help yourself.

CARRIE Remember, Gus, when Julian and I used to eat out there and you and your sister and brother'd walk past and stare at us, and Julian would go tell Mama we wanted more food, and he'd bring it to you himself?

GUS Yes'm. Came in handy. Just like now.

(*He exits from the porch. He picks up a garden hose and disappears to the rear of the house*)

CARRIE (*Looks at* ANNA) Why did I tell him that about Europe?

ANNA I don't know.

CARRIE Let's get out our travel books this evening and write out all our plans.

ANNA No. Don't let's ever speak about it, until we're ready to go, or think about it, or listen to each other, or tell Gus—I don't want to write things down again.

CARRIE It was you who wanted to wait last time. After the wedding.

ANNA It was you, Carrie

CARRIE For a very good reason. Could we give them a smaller wedding present? Lily is a very rich girl and the one thing a very rich girl knows about is sterling silver. Her mother gave them ten thousand dollars. What would Lily have thought of us?

ANNA I don't know. I don't think she cares about things like that. Lily was so in love with Julian—

CARRIE Oh, I imagine even in love you take time off to count your silver.

CARRIE (*Softly*) We could still go to Europe this year. Do you want to? How much money have we got? Did you make the deposit this week?

ANNA Twenty-eight hundred and forty-three dollars. No, I didn't have time.

CARRIE (*Quickly*) Oh, it's too hot tonight. Should we treat ourselves and go out for supper? It's been so long since we ate in a restaurant. Let's start doing our French lessons again because we'll need them now for the trip— (*She moves to the piano and plays and sings the next speech*) "*Une chambre pour deux dames.*" Have you one room for two ladies? "*Ah non! Trop chère!*" Oh no! Too expensive! "*Merci, M'sieur. Trop chère.*" We'll stay in Paris, of course, for just as long as we want. Then we'll go to Strasbourg, have the famous pâté, and put flowers on the graves of Mama's relatives.

ANNA I'll have the pâté. You put flowers on the graves of Mama's relatives.

CARRIE Remember the night Julian told us about the marriage? He said that night we would all go to Europe together, the way we always planned. Mama would want us to put flowers on the graves in Strasbourg. She would, Anna, and so we must.

ANNA I don't know what the dead would like. Maybe Mama's changed.

CARRIE As soon as we do set a date for departure, I'll have my evening dress fixed. No, I won't. Pink's no good for me now. I've kind of changed color as I got older. You, too. Funny. To change color. "*C'est trop chère, M'sieur.*" I don't want to go if we have to say that all the time.

ANNA We've always said it, we always will say it. And why not?

CARRIE I just think it would be better not to go to Europe right now.

ANNA (*Laughs*) We weren't going.

CARRIE Save enough until we can go real right. That won't take long. Maybe just another year.

ANNA A year is a long time—now.

CARRIE If you want to go, just let's get up and go. (*In sudden, false excitement*) Come on. Let's do. I can't tell you how much I want to go—(*Points to the piano*) That and a good piano. Every time there's a wishbone I say I want a good life for Julian, a piano, a trip to Europe. That's all. You know, even if we can't go to Europe we could afford a little trip to Chicago. The coach fares are very cheap—

ANNA I don't think we should run after Julian and Lily and intrude on their lives.

CARRIE Who's doing that? What an unpleasant idea. (*As* ANNA *starts toward the kitchen*) We haven't got twenty-eight hundred and forty-three dollars. I took out a thousand dollars yesterday and sent it to Chicago. I didn't know then that Julian had moved from the hotel. But I am sure they'll forward the money—I signed the wire with love from Anna and Carrie, so he knows it comes from you, too.

ANNA (*Slowly*) I don't think you should have done that.

CARRIE But I knew you would want to send it—

ANNA How do you know what I would want?

CARRIE (*Slowly, hurt*) Shouldn't I know what you want for Julian? (*When* ANNA *does not answer*) I'm sorry our trip will have to wait a little longer, but—

ANNA I'm sorry, too. But it's not the trip. Nor the money. We are interfering, and we told ourselves we wouldn't.

CARRIE But if he needs money—

ANNA Needs it? Julian has a good business. Why do you think he needs it?

CARRIE He's always needed it. (*Quickly*) I mean I don't mean that. I mean it's because the letter didn't come. Anyway, even people with a good business can use a little money— You think I did wrong?

ANNA Yes, I do.
(*She exits*)

CARRIE (*Calling after* ANNA) Julian won't be angry with me. He never has been. I'll just telephone to him and say—(*She makes a half move to the phone*) But there's no place to phone to. Anna, what do you think?

(*There is no answer. After a second she moves back to the piano and begins to play. During her speech* ALBERTINE PRINE *and* HENRY SIMPSON *appear in the garden.* ALBERTINE PRINE *is a handsome woman of about forty-five, dressed with elegance, but in no current fashion. She speaks carefully, as if she were not used to talking very much. Her movements are graceful and quiet.* HENRY *is a colored man of about forty-five. He is dressed in a summer suit, but he carries a chauffeur's cap.* MRS. PRINE *stops as she hears the piano*)

ALBERTINE Is the older one Miss Caroline?

HENRY (*Laughs*) They call her Carrie. No. Miss Anna is the older one.

ALBERTINE (*Smiles*) You laugh at me. But I only met them twice before the marriage. Two long dinners. Many savage tribes have a law that people must eat alone, in silence. Sensible, isn't it? (*She moves toward the porch steps, then stops*) Perhaps it would be best if you went in. I'm not good at seeing people any more, and there will be much chatter. (*He doesn't answer her. She laughs*) Very well. But I am sure it's hot in there. Would you tell them I'm out here?

HENRY (*Gently*) *You* have come to call on *them*.

ALBERTINE Nice to live this close to the river. I still like it down here. Soggy and steaming. The flowers aren't strong enough to cover the river smells. That's the way it should be. Very vain of flowers to compete with the Mississippi. My grandmother lived on this street when I was a little girl, and I liked it then. I used to pretend I slept under the river, and had a secret morning door up into this street. What are you holding?

HENRY A chauffeur's cap.

ALBERTINE You win many small battles. Never mind. Wear it if you must. Put it on now and say I am here.

HENRY No. Just go and ring the bell.

(*She smiles and moves up the porch steps.* ANNA *comes back into the room, dressed in an apron and carrying a tray*)

ANNA (*To* CARRIE) I'm making jambalaya for you.

CARRIE Isn't that nice?

(*The bell rings.* CARRIE *jumps and runs to the door*)

ALBERTINE (*To* CARRIE) Hello, Miss Anna.

CARRIE (*Amazed*) Mrs. Prine. Mrs. Prine. Do come in. (*She moves ahead of* ALBERTINE, *calling*) Mrs. Prine is here. Isn't that nice?

ANNA (*Moves forward*) Mrs. Prine, it's gracious of you to come. We should have come to call on you.

CARRIE (*Flustered*) We're relatives now, after all. We did phone, three times. But, of course, you never got the messages.

ALBERTINE (*To* CARRIE) Yes, I did get them, Miss Anna.

ANNA *I* am Anna.

ALBERTINE Forgive me.

ANNA (*Turns to* CARRIE) And this is Carrie. Close your dress.

CARRIE Oh, my goodness. (*She turns away and nervously buttons her dress*) You must forgive me—

ANNA How are you, Mrs. Prine? Are you spending the summer across the lake?

ALBERTINE No. I've closed the lake house. Now that Lily is married, I stay right here in summer. I don't like the country.

CARRIE Not like the country. My. I never heard anybody say a thing like that before. It takes courage to just up and say you don't like the country. Everybody likes the country.

ALBERTINE Do they? I see so few people.

ANNA (*Quickly*) You must be lonely without Lily.

ALBERTINE No.

CARRIE Oh. Goodness.

ALBERTINE I've come at your supper time—

ANNA And we'd like to share it with you.

CARRIE Oh, please do stay. I'll just go and primp myself—

ALBERTINE No, thank you. I eat at midnight. It's my bad habit to live at night and sleep the days away.

CARRIE Lily said that— Well, she just said that.

ALBERTINE I suppose it was hard on a child, a young girl, not to have her mother available during the day. But perhaps it was just as well. What time do you expect Lily and Julian?

CARRIE Expect them? Expect them? We haven't heard for seventeen days—

ALBERTINE Lily left a message that they'd be here tonight. I came to say—

ANNA (*As* CARRIE *turns to her*) They'd be *here* tonight? We've had no word, Mrs. Prine.

CARRIE (*In great excitement*) The Chicago train comes in at seven. Have we time to get to the station? I'll phone. It's never on time. I'll get dressed right away. Are there enough shrimps? Is there crayfish bisque left? We can still buy some wine—Get dressed, Anna—

ALBERTINE Miss Carrie, they are not on the Chicago train.

CARRIE You said you had a message—

ALBERTINE Yes, Lily spoke with Henry on the phone. She said they would be coming here tonight.

CARRIE Then they *must* be on that train—

ALBERTINE No. The call was not from Chicago. The call came from here.

CARRIE (*Carefully*) It could not have come from here.

ALBERTINE I am sure of it, Miss Carrie, because I saw Lily two nights ago.



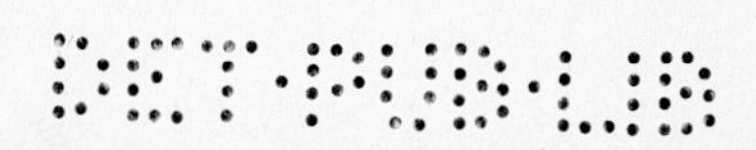

CARRIE Saw her? Here? Here? (*After a second*) What did Lily say?

ALBERTINE I didn't speak to her. She was moving back and forth in front of the house as if she wished to come in and didn't wish to come in.

CARRIE (*After a pause*) You saw your daughter, after a whole year, walking in front of your house and you didn't speak to her? I don't understand, Mrs. Prine.

ALBERTINE That's quite all right.

ANNA (*Softly*) But we need to understand.

ALBERTINE (*Turns her head, looks at* CARRIE *and then at* ANNA) Strange. Sometimes I can't tell which of you is speaking. (*To* CARRIE) Your manner, Miss Carrie, is so, well, so Southern. And then, suddenly, you are saying what I had thought Miss Anna might say. It is as if you had exchanged faces, back and forth, forth and back.

CARRIE (*Sharply*) Did you see Julian?

ALBERTINE There. That's what I mean. No. Julian was not with Lily. I have simply had a message saying they would be here this evening. I have told you all I know.

CARRIE (*To* ANNA) What should we do? (*To* ALBERTINE) What are you going to do?

ALBERTINE I will go home now and ask you to tell Lily that I will come again in the morning. Please tell them that the house is mostly closed up, but by tomorrow I can make them comfortable.

CARRIE Oh, no. Julian will want to be here.

ALBERTINE Ah, I am sure they prefer to stay here, but—

ANNA There must be a good reason why Julian hasn't told us he is in town. If we seem upset, Mrs. Prine, it is because we are not accustomed to—

ALBERTINE —daughters who walk in the night and mothers who do not speak to daughters who walk in the night. I really don't know why Lily didn't come in to me, nor why I didn't ask her. Good night. Thank you. (*She moves out, followed by* ANNA, *followed by a dazed* CARRIE. HENRY *is waiting in the garden.* ALBERTINE *moves toward him, then turns toward the porch*) I think you have met Henry Simpson. Miss Anna and Miss Carrie Berniers, Henry.

HENRY Good evening.

(ALBERTINE *takes his arm and they exit*)

CARRIE (*Softly*) Is *that* the man Lily calls Henry? *That* man was there in a white coat when we went for dinner, but I didn't know that was the Henry. You mean he's a nigger? I never heard anybody introduce a nigger before. I'm sorry I didn't say something. I never think of things in time. (*She turns, sees* ANNA *has gone back to the living room, and moves to join her*) That man Lily called Henry is a nigger. Is he a chauffeur? What is he? Last time, he was a butler. Introduces us to a nigger—(*Sits down, desperate*) Do you believe that strange woman? Do you believe they're in town?

ANNA Maybe Lily's pregnant. They arrived and wanted to go to a doctor first so they could tell us the good news. I'm sure something like that—

CARRIE She's not pregnant.

ANNA How do you know?

CARRIE Girls like Lily don't have babies right away. Too full of good times the first year of marriage, I can tell you that.

ANNA What do you know about the first year of marriage?

CARRIE I just know.

ANNA How? From books you don't read any more?

CARRIE You're saying that again. Teasing me again. No, I don't read much any more, and I don't play the piano, or put ice on my face, or walk for wild flowers—(*Very loudly, as if she were going to cry*) I get tired now after work and that terrible man. All I want to do is have a little something to eat and play casino, and— Don't you like to play casino with me, is that what you're saying?

ANNA Not every night. I like to read—

CARRIE You don't ever have to play casino again. Read whenever you like, but don't nag me about it. You used to do it with Julian, too. Some people read and some people learn other ways— I think she's crazy, that Mrs. Prine. And you know what? I don't believe they're in New Orleans without coming here. (*Lamely*) Do you? What do you think?

ANNA I think it's happened again. And he feels bad and doesn't want to tell us.

CARRIE Well, that's natural enough. Who wants to come home and say they've failed? What do you mean? *What's* happened again?

ANNA (*Gently*) You understand me.

(*She rises and exits toward the kitchen*)

CARRIE I don't think it's nice of us to guess this way. We don't know anything, and yet here we are—(*But* ANNA *has left the room*) A great many men take a long time to find themselves. And a lot of *good* business men just aren't worth bowing to. Goodness. Look at the people in my office. Dull, stupid—ugly, too. I don't like ugly people. I just can't help it, and I'm not ashamed any more to say it. (ANNA *comes back carrying a tray of food*) Are you going to *eat?*

ANNA I always have. I think it's best to continue.

CARRIE You're just as worried and nervous as I am. You always talk cold when you get nervous. Anna. Please. When he comes, don't be cold. Please. It will hurt him—

ANNA Why do you so often make it seem as if I had always been severe and unloving? I don't think it's true.

CARRIE I don't believe I do that. It's you who gave him everything, long before I was old enough to help. But sometimes you go away from us both, and, well, it worries Julian when you do that.

ANNA (*Takes a bankbook from her pocket*) Here is the savings bankbook. Give it to him.

CARRIE (*Deeply pleased*) Oh, thank you. I'll give it to him when we're alone and Lily doesn't see. (ANNA *sits at the table, and puts food on* CARRIE's *plate.* CARRIE *moves about*) It's only for a short time. We'll have it back. After all, in a sense, this money is his. We lent it to him and he paid us back. This is the very money he paid us back, Anna. So, in a sense, its his.

ANNA Do come and eat.

CARRIE You're thinking that what I just said is foolish. You're thinking that you never understood where he got the money to pay for your operation—

ANNA You know very well were he got it: He played in a dangerous poker game.

CARRIE I'm not so sure. I often wondered—

ANNA The shrimps are getting cold (*She begins to eat*)

CARRIE I can't eat. I don't know how you can. (*Sighs, then brightens*) You know, it sounds strange, but I am positive he will make a fortune someday.

ANNA A fortune isn't necessary. A job is.

CARRIE All those self-made men at the office. Like Mr. Barrett. No interest in anything. Making fun of opera and poetry and women. Mean, too, ever since he tried to put his hands on me years ago. Pig. Things can go wrong for a long time and then suddenly everything in a man's life clears up— Have you a headache, Anna? Do your eyes worry you tonight? Can I get you something?

ANNA I haven't a headache. And if I had I wouldn't know the remedy. A prescription put up fresh each time Julian fails.

CARRIE Oh, don't be sad. I'm not. I feel cheerful. Place and people and time make things go wrong, and then all of a sudden—(*There is the offstage noise of a car. She jumps up, runs to the window, stares out, nods at what she sees. Slowly, suddenly cool and calm, she turns back to* ANNA) I am going to wait on the porch. Please don't show what you feel. Welcome him as he should always be welcomed in this, his house.

(*She moves to the porch.* JULIAN'S *voice is heard offstage*)

JULIAN Is that my Carrie on the porch?

CARRIE (*Laughs with enormous pleasure*) Yes, that's your Carrie on the porch. I can still jump. Shall I jump and you will catch me? (*In the middle of her speech, as she begins a jump movement, a* TAXI DRIVER *appears carrying a very large number of packages and valises*) Oh.

(JULIAN and LILY BERNIERS *appear. He is a handsome, tall man of about thirty-four.* LILY *is a frail, pretty girl of about twenty-one. She moves behind him.* JULIAN'S *arms and hands are filled with valises and packages*)

JULIAN Don't jump. I have no hands to catch you. (*Grinning, he moves up the steps as* CARRIE *waits for him. He puts the valises down and takes her in his arms, lifting her from the ground*) Darling Carrie-Pie.

CARRIE Julian.

(*He kisses her, puts her down. She clings to him a minute and follows him as he moves quickly into the house and toward* ANNA. LILY *follows* CARRIE. ANNA *stands waiting for him, smiling warmly. When he kisses* ANNA *it is quite different—no less warm, but different—from his greeting to* CARRIE. ANNA *moves away from him and toward* LILY)

ANNA My dear Lily, how good to see you.

CARRIE (*To* JULIAN) One year and six days. (*As she hears* ANNA's *greeting to* LILY) Lily! I didn't see you. (*Kisses* LILY. LILY *smiles and kisses her*) Forgive me. One year and six days. I was so excited that I didn't see you—

JULIAN (*To the* TAXI DRIVER, *who comes in carrying the valises and packages*) Bring them in. Bring them in. I'm hungry, Anna. Hungry for your cooking. Not a good restaurant in Chicago. Would *not* know a red pepper if they saw one.

CARRIE There's crayfish in the icebox, thank God, and jambalaya on the table—

JULIAN Then go and get them. I'm weak. *Very,* very weak.

ANNA (*Laughs*) You don't look it.

CARRIE Sit down, dear—

(*She starts to run off to the kitchen. Before she does,* JULIAN *hands the* TAXI DRIVER *several bills. She peers at them.* JULIAN *laughs*)

JULIAN Don't be nosey. He deserves them. No porters at the station because the train came in early.

TAXI DRIVER (*Stares at the bills*) Thank you, sir. Thank you— (*Puzzled*) The train came in—

JULIAN (*Quickly*) All right. Good-bye. (*Gives him another bill*) Buy your baby something from me.

TAXI DRIVER Thank you, sir. But I have to say in frank and complete honesty that I haven't got a baby.

JULIAN (*Gives him another bill*) Then take this and get one and name it Julian.

(*The* TAXI DRIVER *laughs and exits*)

ANNA You still say that to waiters and taxi drivers? That means you've been in a poker game. And what train came in early?

CARRIE (*Very quickly*) Anna, go get the crayfish. And make fresh, hot coffee. Lily, shall I take you to your room? Oh, my no, it needs cleaning. Well, just sit down. Anna, get the crayfish for Julian.

ANNA There are no crayfish.

JULIAN (*Is eating the dinner on the table with great pleasure*) We'll go out later and have them with champagne. (*To* ANNA) The same dress?

ANNA The same dress. You look tired, Lily. Can I get you something?

LILY I am tired. Julian doesn't like me to be tired.

JULIAN I don't like anybody to be tired. But it was a long trip, darling— (*As if he is prompting her*) Wasn't it a long trip, Lily?

LILY Yes. When it happened. It was long when it happened.

JULIAN Lily.

LILY (*Quickly, to* CARRIE *and* ANNA) It was a very long trip. Longer than going.

ANNA The wedding day. My how it rained. And Julian put his new coat round your pretty dress and the drawing room was full of flowers. Remember?

LILY (*Smiling, suddenly uplifted, happy*) Did it rain? I don't remember. It was all days to me: Cold and hot days, fog and light, and I was on a high hill running down with the top of me, and flying with the left of me, and singing with the right of me—(*Softly, as if she is worn out*) I was doing everything nice anybody had ever done nice.

ANNA (*Touched*) Nice.

LILY What were you doing when I was doing all that, Julian?

JULIAN (*His mouth very full*) Being my kind of happy.

LILY You're always happy.

JULIAN I am glad you think that, darling.

ANNA You've given us no news, How is the shoe factory?

JULIAN What shoe factory?

(*There is a long silence. He is grinning and eating.* ANNA *moves toward the window, and takes in a plant.* CARRIE, *standing behind* JULIAN, *holds up her hand in an attempt to stop* ANNA's *questions.* ANNA *sees it and ignores it*)

ANNA (*Carefully*) The shoe factory that you bought in Chicago.

JULIAN Oh, *that* shoe factory. It's gone.

ANNA Don't be flip with me, Julian.

CARRIE (*Gesturing wildly*) He's not. He's just trying to explain—

JULIAN (*Turns, sees* CARRIE, *laughs, catches the gesturing hand*) No, I'm not. I'm not trying to explain anything. (*To* ANNA) I was being flip. I forget that you worry about the money I lose.

ANNA It's not the money—It's that you don't seem to care. And the money was—

JULIAN Lily's money.

LILY My money? Doesn't matter about my money. I don't want money.

CARRIE (*To* LILY) You mustn't worry about it. Not worth it.

LILY I'm not worried about money, Miss Carrie.

CARRIE I suppose rich people always worry about money. People like us have to learn there are more important things.

LILY I said I wasn't worried about money, Miss Carrie.

CARRIE Well, you mustn't.

JULIAN (*To* ANNA) The factory was a crooked sell. The machinery wasn't any good. I didn't know anything about shoe machinery and I never should have thought I did. Man who sold it to me faked the books. That's all.

CARRIE (*Softly*) That could happen to anybody.

JULIAN (*Laughs*) No. Not to anybody. Just me.

CARRIE That's not true. And you mustn't ever believe it.

JULIAN Darling Carrie. Hiding her hopes that I would come home with Chicago over my shoulder, dressed in pure gold, bringing candied oranges to hang in your hair. Well, that's just what I've done. Your hair don't look nice, Carrie-Pie.

ANNA (*Rises, crosses to the pile of dishes to carry them out*) We can help you.

CARRIE Yes, indeed we can. Julian, come in the kitchen and help me wash the dishes.

JULIAN No, ma'am. And you're never going to wash dishes again.

ANNA I don't wish to ask questions that you might not like, Julian. But it's uncomfortable this way. Your mother was here, Lily. She said she had seen you, had a message from you. She said she would come back tomorrow. (*To* JULIAN, *who has turned to stare at* LILY) So this is not your first night in town. You need not explain, but I thought we should.

JULIAN We've been in New Orleans for a week, at the hotel. I had a good reason for that. It was no neglect of you. I even came by and stared in at you—(*Points outside*)—the first hour back. You were playing casino and Anna was yawning. You look tired, both of you. You need a long, long good time. (*To* ANNA) This time, no need to be sad. I used to tell you: never was any good; never came out anywhere.

ANNA I am sad that you think it all so easy, so unimportant, so—

"Never came out anywhere." I guess not, although I don't think those words mean very much.

CARRIE (*To* ANNA, *in a voice used once before*) I won't have that kind of talk. This is a happy, joyous night. Julian is home and that's all we need to know. It's a happy, joyous night.

(ANNA *exits*)

LILY (*To* JULIAN) I didn't see my mother, I didn't go in. And I only sent the message today. I knew we'd arrive here, anyway, so—(*Softly, when there is no answer*)—I disobeyed you. But not much. Have I done harm?

JULIAN No.

(CARRIE, *listening, pretending she isn't, is idly playing on the piano with one hand*)

LILY I know you told me not to see anybody. But you didn't tell me why or anything. You just kept leaving the hotel. I want to see my mother. I want to talk with my mother.

JULIAN (*Smiles*) I'm glad to hear that. I've never heard you want that before.

LILY Are you angry with me?

JULIAN (*Smiles at her, shakes his head, moves away*) Carrie, stop that awful sound, darling. Just wait for the good piano—

CARRIE (*Laughs*) No, I'd only find out I couldn't really play.

(JULIAN *has moved out to porch and is hauling in valises.* LILY *rises and follows him*)

JULIAN (*Calling to* CARRIE) You all been to the opera?

CARRIE No. We'll wait until Europe.

JULIAN (*Laughs*) Still talking about Europe?

CARRIE Oh, we'll go someday. You'll see.

JULIAN (*Bringing in valises*) Someday soon?
(*He goes out again for more*)

CARRIE In a few years. Plenty of time. We're not that old.
(*She moves quickly out of the room*)

JULIAN Yes, you are. Old enough to have fun. Have to crowd it in now, Carrie, both of you. Crowd it in fast. (*Smiling at* LILY) You, too. Twenty-one is very, very old.

LILY (*She has followed him to the porch*) Tell me you're not angry with me.

JULIAN (*His arms heavy with valises*) I am not angry with you. Have I ever been angry with you? Why do you ask me that so often?

LILY (*As she steps aside*) Julian, who is the lady you talked to on the train?

JULIAN (*Too lightly*) Which lady?—I talk to everybody.

LILY The not such a young lady with the sad face.

JULIAN Most ladies on trains are not so young and have sad faces. I often wondered why. (*He tries to pass her*) Move, darling.

LILY The one you were with today and yesterday and—

JULIAN (*Turns, stares at her*) Where did you see me?

LILY I don't know. Just on the street. In front of the hotel—

JULIAN No, you didn't.

LILY No, I didn't. That's the first lie I ever told you, Julian.

JULIAN Then it's one more than I ever told you.
(*Carrying the valises, he moves into the living room.* LILY *follows him*)

LILY I saw you in Audubon Park. On a bench. By the ducks.

JULIAN Have you told anybody?

LILY No.

JULIAN Don't. The lady would be in trouble. And so would we.

LILY And in that little restaurant. At a table—

JULIAN Oh, Lily.

LILY I didn't mean to walk after you, to follow you. But I was so lonely in the hotel room, locked up the way you asked me to be.

JULIAN All right, darling, all right. Don't follow me, Lily, ever again. That's not the way to be married. (LILY *hesitates, as if to say something, then exits*) Hey, everybody. Come and get your presents. Hey, where is everybody?

CARRIE (*Appears in the garden, runs up the porch, speaks in a whisper*) Julian. I want to speak to you. Come here.

JULIAN Can't. You come here.

CARRIE Sssssh. (*He comes to the porch. She sits down on the porch steps*) Come here. I've got a nice secret. And this is where we always told nice secrets.

JULIAN You come here. *I* got nice secrets. Where's Anna? Anna!

CARRIE Ssh. Ssh.

JULIAN (*Sits beside her*) What's the matter with you?

CARRIE (*Gives him the savings bankbook*) No need for Lily to see. You'll just tell her it's yours. More than twenty-eight hundred dollars. And we don't need any of it, not any of it, so don't say anything—(*He takes her hands, kisses them. She is very moved. Softly, embarrassed*) Don't say anything, please. And if that isn't enough, we can manage other things, too.

JULIAN (*Stares at the book, then rises and calls out*) Anna!

CARRIE Anna doesn't want any thanks—

(ANNA *comes into the room*)

JULIAN (*Enters the room, holds out the bankbook*) God bless you. All my life it's been this way.

ANNA (*Smiles*) You are our life. It is we who should thank you.

(*He takes her in his arms*)

JULIAN How many, many times?

CARRIE (*Comes into the room*) You paid it back, always.

JULIAN You know I didn't. But this time I will.

CARRIE Of course you will. But Lily doesn't have to know about all this— So ssh.

JULIAN Stop ssshing me and come here and sit down and stop talking. (*He puts* CARRIE *in a chair and motions to* ANNA *to be seated. Then he leans down to unwrap the boxes and open the valises. The boxes are dressmaker boxes, and he pulls from them two fancy evening dresses. They are too grand for anything less than a ball.* CARRIE *leans forward, stares at them*) For a ball. Wear them the second time at the opera, if you like. But I don't think dresses like these should be worn twice in the same city, do you? Everybody in Paris will talk, and we can't have that. (*He opens another box*) Maybe you can wear them again when you get to Strasbourg. (*Points his finger at* CARRIE) Not to the cemetery. I bet the opera house there is drafty—(*He has taken out two fur pieces and arranged them over the dresses*) No, No. I've got things mixed up. (*He begins to fumble in another box*) Or so the lady said. The furs are for breakfast or something. (*He is now holding up two fur-trimmed opera coats. They are royal in feeling*) These are for the dresses. And maybe they can be worn the second time. (*He moves to arrange them over* ANNA *and* CARRIE. CARRIE's *is much too large and she looks drowned. He points to the other boxes and valises*) Suits for traveling. Dresses for informal evenings, whatever that is. (*Pulls out frothy, very youthful negligees*) For flirtations on Italian terraces. (*Drapes them over* ANNA *and* CARRIE. *He goes to* CARRIE *with a large rather flashy necklace*) Garnets. Your birthstone. Next time, pearls. (*He drapes over* ANNA's *arm a large gold mesh bag*) Remember when old lady Senlis used to come along swinging her gold mesh bag, and your eyes would pop out wondering what was in it? Look and see what's in this one.

ANNA (*Softly*) What is all this, Julian?

JULIAN It is that we're rich. Just open your gold mesh bag with diamond initials—Anna, *diamond* initials—and see what's inside.

CARRIE (*Loud, nervous giggle*) The only thing could be, is a certificate to an insane asylum.

JULIAN (*Takes an envelope from the purse*) You're wrong. A certificate to a boat called the *Ottavia,* sailing day after tomorrow. Two rooms, one of them a parlor. Think of that, a parlor on a boat. (*He takes the envelope to* CARRIE) Look at it, look at it. Of course, we had always planned to go together. But I won't be able to go with you, darling, not this time, big business here, and all that. But we'll join you in a few months—

CARRIE (*Dully*) We'll wait for you.

JULIAN No, you won't. No more waiting for anything.

ANNA (*Softly*) Where does all this come from, Julian?

JULIAN All over town. I just went in places and said bring out the best for two pretty ladies who are on their way. On their way.

ANNA You know what I mean.

JULIAN I know what you mean. They were bought with my money. Mine. Yours. Ours. We're rich. How do you like that, how do you like it?

CARRIE We'll like it fine—when it happens. (*Giggles*) Rich. Us!

Anne Revere, Jason Robards, Jr., and Maureen Stapleton,
as ANNA, JULIAN and CARRIE BERNIERS

JULIAN What are you doing?

CARRIE Trying to make a neat package.

JULIAN Stop it. (*When she doesn't*) I said to stop it. Nothing's going back this time. Listen to me. Now listen to me. We're rich. (LILY *comes into the room. She is in her slip and is carrying a hairbrush. He smiles at her*) Aren't we rich?

LILY Mama's rich, I guess.

JULIAN No, us, us. I've been telling you for a week.

LILY There are three men at the back door. From a trucking company—

JULIAN Tell them to bring them in, darling. (*She exits*) Right in here. Now you're going to see something.

CARRIE (*Stares at the boat tickets*) Are these real boat tickets? I mean, stamped and bought?

JULIAN Bought and stamped. Look. It's going to be this way. The first money is for us to have things. Have fun. After that, I promise you, we'll invest. And like all people with money, we'll make more and more and more until we get sick from it. Rich people get sick more than we do. Maybe from worry.

ANNA Poor people, too. Like me, right now. (*Very sharply*) Where did you get this money, Julian?

CARRIE Oh, now don't start that tone. You know very well he's been in a poker game.

JULIAN No, she doesn't know that, and you don't either. (*Two* MOVING MEN *appear, carrying a fancy, highly carved spinet. There is a big sign on the spinet lettered* CARRIE) Come in. Just put it down. (*Motions to* CARRIE) By that lady.

(The MEN *carry the spinet to* CARRIE *and place it near her*)

CARRIE My God.

(*Another* MOVING MAN *comes in wheeling a large refrigerator on a dolly. The first two* MEN *move to help him*)

JULIAN And put that by this lady (*He motions toward* ANNA. *They wheel the refrigerator and place it almost in front of* ANNA. LILY *comes back into the room*) Good. (*He pulls out several large bills*) Thank you. Buy the babies something from me. (*To the head* MOVING MAN) Name the next one Julian.

MOVING MAN There ain't going to be no next one. Thank you.

(*They exit*)

LILY Why do you always say that? We'll name our son Julian. Don't you believe—

JULIAN (*Laughs*) Insurance. That's all.

CARRIE (*To* LILY) You're in your slip. In front of men.

JULIAN Can't harm them.

CARRIE I never heard of such a thing. Answering the door in your underwear. Don't you mind?

JULIAN I mind that you haven't looked at your piano. Think, Carrie, a fine new piano, what you always wanted, right in front of you— Play it. Play it for me, Carrie, the way we used to always say.

*(She puts out her hand, touches a note, takes her hand away and puts it over her face)*

JULIAN *(Softly, smiling)* I know. Take your time.

ANNA What is all this? Answer me, please, Julian.

JULIAN I'm going to tell you all about it someday soon. I can't now. But I'll tell you this much, I didn't play poker. All I did was sell some real estate.

ANNA You never owned any real estate.

JULIAN No. But I do now, see?

ANNA No, I don't see. I don't see at all.

JULIAN Once I liked somebody and they liked me, and she thought I was kind to her. So years go by and she hears about a good thing, and gives me the tip on it. And the tip works. Boy, how it worked. Now let it go. I'll tell you soon, but in the meantime I gave my word because she could be in bad trouble. Now stop worrying, and sit back—*(He guides* ANNA's *hand to refrigerator door, opens it, pulls an envelope from it)* I finished the deal and collected the money at two o'clock today. At two-eighteen, I rang the bells of Mr. Maxwell Shine. And so here's the mortgage to the house. *(Kneels; softly)* Look, Anna, first time in our lives, first time in our father's life. You have a house, without worry or asking him to wait. Remember when I was a kid and the time you took me with you and you made me tell Mr. Shine how I wouldn't have anyplace to live unless— Christ God, how I hated— Do you remember?

ANNA I remember.

JULIAN Well, there'll never be such things to say again. Not for any of us. (*He rises and shouts*) Not ever, ever. (*To* CARRIE) I wrote your Mr. Barrett a letter last night. I wrote it three times. "Your petty angers, the silk stockings at Christmas that were always cheaper than a decent salary. Miss Caroline Berniers will not return to work." (CARRIE *rises, makes a sound in her throat, stands staring at him. He turns to* ANNA) For you I just wrote that Miss Anna Berniers was resigning from the coat department because she was leaving for an extended European tour. (*He sits down.* ANNA *lifts her head and stares at him. There is a long silence*) Well. Say something.

ANNA I can't say something.

JULIAN I know, I know. All came so fast. Well, we don't have to say things to each other, never did. Just sit back and have fun. That's all I want. (*To* LILY) And for you— Give me the wedding ring. (*Sharply she pulls back from him*) Give it to me. (*He takes the ring from her finger*) Twenty dollars in a pawnshop, and I polished it, and prayed you wouldn't mind, or say anything. (*He takes from his pocket, and puts on her finger, a very large diamond ring*) With this, I you wed again, and forever.

LILY Please give me my ring.

JULIAN (*Now he holds up her hand so that she can see her new diamond ring*) Look, darling, look at it. Superstitious? (*He looks at* LILY, *then at* CARRIE, *then at* ANNA) Please don't cry or look it, all of you. (*He takes an envelope from his pocket, goes to each of them as he speaks, lets them look into the envelope*) One hundred and fifty thousand dollars, less peanuts—(*Motions to the packages*)—for this. Seventy-five thousand for my partner, seventy-five thousand for me. My lawyer said I shouldn't carry all that cash around, rich people don't carry cash, not more than ten or twenty dollars, so other people pay the bills. But I said I'll carry this, I like it— Hey, did you hear—my lawyer. *I've* got a *lawyer*. What do you think of that? (CARRIE *has paid little attention to the money in the envelope, but* ANNA *is staring at it*) Ain't counterfeit. Twenty, five thousand dollar bills; fifty, one thousand dollar bills— You'll believe it all by tomorrow. Big, successful Julian, the way you wanted me. The man who was never good at anything except living on his sisters, and losing his wife's money. I never minded failure much, you minded. But you know what? I like things this way: Making bargains, talking big— I don't take my hat off in elevators any more—(*Laughs with great pleasure and picks up a large package*) Now to *important* business. Last night I drew up a budget list, you know, the way we used to. Only where we put carfare for the week, I put champagne, and where we put lunch money, sixty cents each, I put caviar. You'll like caviar.

CARRIE I hate caviar. The one time I ever ate it, I hated it. Just hated it.

JULIAN (*Holds up the package*) Champagne. *And* caviar, Carrie-Pie. You'll learn to like it. (*He starts toward the kitchen*) We're going to have a champagne-caviar party just for us. Sit down and play the piano.

(*He exits*)

CARRIE (*Softly*) Since when do you give me orders? (*Very loudly*) I said since when do you give me orders? (ANNA *puts up a hand, as if to quiet her*) I don't believe it all. I don't believe it. (*When* ANNA *doesn't answer her*) We have no jobs. (*To* LILY) What is this all about?

LILY I want my ring. I was married in my ring.

CARRIE I asked you a question, Lily.

LILY I didn't hear you.

CARRIE What is this all about? Where did Julian get this money?

LILY I don't know, ma'am. A lady came to Chicago and phoned him, and he went to see her, and everything changed and he said we were coming here, and she was on the train, and he didn't want me to know. She calls him every night at six o'clock.

CARRIE I'm not talking about women. That's not my business. I'm talking about this—(*She motions around*) Europe day after tomorrow! Has he gone crazy? What does he think we are, fine ladies with maids and secretaries who can move whenever they like? Whore's clothes. I wouldn't be seen in this. Not seen in them. (*Turns on* ANNA) For God's sake take off that stuff. What are you doing?

ANNA (*Who is reading the mortgage document*) Trying to understand.

CARRIE (*In a whisper*) Does it really say—

ANNA Yes. It really says we own this house.

CARRIE This house. This awful house. He's changed. He even talks different. Didn't he know we hated this house, always, always, always.

ANNA You used to tell him how much we liked it, and the garden, and the street, and the memories of Mama and Papa.

CARRIE You know very well I said all that to keep him from being ashamed of the house and what we didn't have—

ANNA (*Hands her the paper*) Well. We've been rewarded.

LILY I want my ring. I was married in my ring. (*She holds up her hand*) This is a vulgar ring.

CARRIE (*Points to a tiny pin she is wearing*) Topaz is my birthstone. How could he forget when he gave me this pin with the first job he ever lost. I even wear it at night—

LILY I want my married ring.

CARRIE You said that before.

(LILY *runs toward the table, picks up the ring. As she does, the phone rings, and she continues the run that will bring her to the phone*)

LILY Hello. (*A slight pause*) No, ma'am. No, he isn't. This is his wife. What is *your* name?

(*She stares at the phone and then hangs up. After a second, she puts on the old ring and, with a violent movement, throws the diamond toward the window. It hits the window and drops.* JULIAN *comes into the room carrying an ice bucket, two bottles of champagne, glasses and two very large jars of caviar*)

JULIAN I heard the phone. Didn't the phone ring?

ANNA (*After a second*) No.

JULIAN (*Pouring*) Now. (*To* CARRIE, *points to the piano*) Why aren't you playing? And you took off— Put the pretty clothes on so I can be proud.

CARRIE (*Sharply*) All of them?

LILY The phone did ring. It was that lady who calls every evening. I told her you weren't here. I don't know why I said it, but I did.

JULIAN I have business with that lady. I've told you that before. I was to meet her this evening. It's not easy for her to call me and I can't call her. Did she say she'd call back tonight? (LILY *shakes her head*) Why did you tell her I wasn't here?

LILY I didn't know I was going to do it. Please forgive me. It wasn't nice.

JULIAN Not nice, wasn't it? You know what I think it wasn't? Respectful. (*He moves toward* CARRIE) Re-spect-ful— Respectful. I don't think I can spell that word. I never used it before. But I like it. (*He hits his chest*) A man. Respect. That's what you always said, success isn't everything but it makes a man stand straight, and you were right. (*He hands a glass of champagne to* ANNA *and offers caviar. He speaks to* CARRIE) You want to know something? I bring you a piano, I ask you to play it for me, you don't. I don't think that's respectful. (*He laughs*) I like that word. (CARRIE *sits down at the piano and begins to play. She fumbles, as if she is thinking of something else, then plays a waltz.* JULIAN *moves to* LILY, *gives her a glass, whirls her around, kisses her hair*) I forgive you, my infant bride. (*He looks at her hand*) Where's your ring?

(ANNA *rises, crosses, and picks up the the ring*)

LILY I don't know.

JULIAN You don't know?

ANNA I have it. I was looking at it.

(JULIAN *smiles, kisses* LILY'S *hair. The music stops sharply and he turns to* CARRIE)

JULIAN More, more. It's a party. We're having a party. (*To* ANNA) Dance?

(*He pulls her to her feet, whirls her around, the long evening coat tangled in her legs*)

CARRIE Anna. You look like a fool. Like a real fool.

JULIAN What's the matter? (*Moving to* CARRIE. *He hands her a glass of champagne. Staring at him, she sips it*) Good? (*He spoons out a large amount of caviar, sings*) *Avez-vous les chambres, Monsieur Hotel-keeper? Non, ils ne sont pas trop chères.*" Nothing is too expensive now. Send up two pounds *de* caviar *pour* breakfast *pour ma soeur et moi.* (*He leans over her with the caviar*) Now.

(*He forces her mouth open.* JULIAN *laughs*)

CARRIE You're laughing at me. You've never laughed at me before. (*She rises, shrilly*) You're laughing at me.

JULIAN No, I wasn't. I'm just happy. I'm giving a party—(*He looks at* ANNA, *who has her head hung; at* LILY, *who looks sad and tearful*) What's the matter with everybody? (*He drinks his champagne. He pours himself another drink, bolts it, stares at them*) We're not having a very nice party. What's the matter?

*Curtain*

# ACT TWO

## ACT TWO

*Early Thursday morning. The spinet and the refrigerator are as they were the night before.* ANNA, *in a housedress, is lowering the plants from the window into the garden. On a chair is a large, old-fashioned trunk-type suitcase; near the suitcase are two pairs of shoes.* ANNA *sits down, and begins to polish the shoes with rag and paste.* CARRIE *enters carrying a coffee pot. She is dressed and has on her hat. She sits down and pours herself a cup of coffee.*

CARRIE Is your headache better?

ANNA I didn't have a headache.

CARRIE You said you did.

ANNA No, I didn't.

CARRIE Last night, before you went to bed, you said your eyes were bothering you, you had a headache.

ANNA No.

CARRIE I think everybody's going crazy. I really do. No wonder you can't remember what you said. I don't think I slept an hour. I'd close my eyes, and say I don't believe it, when I get up —(*Points to the spinet, the boxes, etc.*)—that thing, and that, won't be there, and it will be years ago. He stayed out in the garden drinking by himself till late last night. (*Points inside*) Still asleep?

ANNA I suppose so.

CARRIE How could *you* have slept last night? Mama used to say you could sleep through anything.

ANNA Mama believed that lack of sleep was a sign of good breeding. Do you remember the time she said she hadn't slept for two years? (*Points inside*) Yes, I heard Lily, if that's what you mean.

CARRIE She rattled around half the night. She went out, she came back, she went out. She's a very strange girl. I remember thinking that the first time I ever met her. (*Points around the room*) And she doesn't know any more about all this than we do. That's not natural in a good marriage. In a good marriage a man doesn't have secrets from his wife.

ANNA How do you know?

CARRIE It's not natural in a good marriage, I can tell you that.

ANNA We don't know anything about a good marriage or a bad one. I read somewhere that old maids are the true detectives of the human heart. But I don't want to be a detective of other people's hearts. I'm having enough trouble with my own.

CARRIE I know you are. I know you're just as worried as I am. I know that's why you're having headaches again.

ANNA I said I didn't have a headache.

CARRIE I'll get you something for it. Julian pampers Lily as if she were a child. He never treated us that way, always boasted of our good sense.

ANNA He didn't marry us.

CARRIE Nobody wants a child for a wife.

ANNA There's no sense telling your opinions about marriage to me. I don't know anything about it.

*(She gets up, carries a pair of shoes to the valise, wraps them in paper, and packs them)*

CARRIE What are you doing?

ANNA Put your clothes out. I'm going to wash and iron today.

CARRIE What for?

ANNA *(Turns to stare at her)* Europe.

CARRIE We'll miss the eight-thirty streetcar. *(When there is no answer)* We'll miss the eight-thirty streetcar. *(When there is no answer)* I know what Julian said. But I get the mail before Mr. Barrett, and if Julian did write such a letter I'll just throw it out. You better go down to the store and get somebody to do the same for you. *(Very sharply, when* ANNA *does not answer)* *We have no jobs.* They're not easy to get and we're not young. You told me all my life what that would mean to us. You said that as long as we could work and save a little then we could get sick when we were old, and take care of Julian, and not end as Mama and Papa did.

ANNA Julian has come home rich. We can get sick now.

CARRIE Rich! Do you really believe this foolishness? Julian rich! God knows what he's been up to. God knows when and how it will blow up. Doesn't it worry you?

ANNA Yes. It worries me. But I think we should go to Europe. He wants us to go.

CARRIE What do you mean, he wants us to go? You make it sound as if we're in his way.

ANNA I don't know what I mean.

CARRIE Go to Europe. What are you talking about? What's going to happen when trouble comes if we're not here to take care of it?

ANNA Why do you think trouble will come?

CARRIE Because it always has. You know very well what I mean. Well, you go to Europe and I'll go to work.

ANNA (*Laughs*) All right.

CARRIE If Mr. Samuel Barrett has seen the letter, I'll apologize. Mr. Barrett likes people to apologize. Nineteen years of faithful work matter for something. (*Giggles*) Ho, ho. I'd like to see you in Europe alone.

(LILY *appears from the bedroom. She has on a dress and over the dress she has on a nightgown. She stares at* CARRIE *and* ANNA *as if she didn't know who they were*)

ANNA Morning. (*She rises to pour* LILY *a cup of coffee*) Julian want his breakfast?

LILY I don't know. (*She points to the left side of the room*) He slept in there.

CARRIE Mama and Papa's room.

LILY He thought I was asleep when he went in there, but I wasn't.

CARRIE No, you certainly weren't. You moved around most of the night. Are you dressed or undressed? Well, I'm off to work.

LILY My. It's awfully hot to go to work.

CARRIE Yes. And sometimes it's awfully cold.

(*She exits toward the porch. As she moves out,* MRS. PRINE *appears in the garden.* HENRY *stands outside the garden fence. During the scene between* LILY *and* ALBERTINE, *he will occasionally be seen moving back and forth*)

ALBERTINE Good morning.

CARRIE Good morning.

(CARRIE *hurries off. At the sound of her mother's voice,* LILY *runs to the porch, stares at her mother and runs back into the room*)

LILY Oh. Where are my shoes? (*Stares down at herself, sees that she is barefoot, hestitates*) Oh. (*Runs out again to the porch and down to the garden*) Mama. I don't know why I did that.

(ALBERTINE *moves toward her and they kiss*)

ALBERTINE I come calling much too early. I forget that other people sleep at night.

LILY I didn't.

ALBERTINE I know.

LILY What did Henry tell you?

ALBERTINE That you were out, er, visiting, and wanted to speak with me.

LILY Yes. I didn't want Henry to come and get me. I didn't need his help.

ALBERTINE He said the neighborhood worried him at two o'clock in the morning.

LILY How did he know where I was?

ALBERTINE You told him on the phone.

LILY Did I? I don't remember— I was mean to Henry. Did he tell you that?

ALBERTINE No.

LILY (*After a second*) I'm sorry I spoke that way.

ALBERTINE How are you, Lily? I haven't seen you in a whole year. The garden wing of the house is being cleaned for you. You are very welcome, and I've come to say that to Julian.

LILY Thank you. It's nice that you want us. Do you?

ALBERTINE You are thinner, Lily. Have you been well?

LILY Do you?

ALBERTINE Do I what?

LILY Do you really want me to come home again?

ALBERTINE I'll come later. You must be tired from your—night's exercise.

LILY (*Quickly*) Mama, don't go. Please. I need help. Your help. I'll start at the start and try not to take long and say things nice and clear—

ALBERTINE There's no need. Don't distress yourself. I've guessed your trouble and I've brought you a check. (*She takes a check from her bag and puts it on the garden table*) Will you and Julian come and dine at eight? Then you'll decide if you wish to move in, or, if in this heat, you prefer the lake house. I've always meant to give you the lake house, Lily, and tomorrow we'll go around and have Warkins do the papers. (*When there is no answer*) At eight?

LILY What does Mrs. Warkins look like? Does she speak in a low voice?

ALBERTINE I don't know. I haven't seen her in years, and then only once or twice.

LILY You haven't seen anybody in years, except Henry, of course. How old is Mrs. Warkins?

ALBERTINE I know little about her, Lily. It's bad enough to

know Warkins. I remember her as a tall woman with a sad face. Possibly from being married to a lawyer.

LILY Is she in love with Mr. Warkins?

ALBERTINE (*Smiles, shrugs*) That is a remarkable idea. Thank God I've never been in a position to find out. Let's waste our time saying things like each to his own taste, and shaking our heads in gossip, but let's do it another time.

LILY Please don't smile and shrug, Mama. It always makes me nervous. You are angry because I was mean to Henry last night, and he told you.

ALBERTINE He told me nothing.

LILY *I was mean to Henry.* That was bad of me, wasn't it?

ALBERTINE (*Wearily, softly*) I don't know.

LILY Well, tell him I'm sorry.

ALBERTINE You have been saying you are sorry, in space, for many years.

LILY You *are* angry now.

ALBERTINE Oh, Lily.

LILY I don't know what makes me speak so wrong. All I want is to tell you, and have you help me. But I get things out of order— Mama, I'm in trouble.

ALBERTINE I know Julian lost the factory. Well, perhaps he doesn't belong in a large city. He'll find something here. In the meantime—(*She picks up the check and hands it to* LILY)

LILY What is it, Mama?

ALBERTINE (*Slowly, too patiently*) I told you. It's a check. A check is for money. Money. It's five thousand dollars. It's yours. Oblige me by not speaking of it again.

LILY Don't be angry with me.

ALBERTINE (*After a second*) Oh, Lily. Something always happens between us.

LILY If I could only speak in order, then I wouldn't—

ALBERTINE Don't fret. Everybody talks too much, too many words, and gets them out of order.

LILY I know you think that. I know you do. That's what makes it so hard. It's that you never talk much, and you look down on people who don't do it very well.

ALBERTINE You said you were in trouble. Do you wish to tell me about it?

LILY You speak so severely, Mama.

ALBERTINE Please, Lily, let us cease this talking about talking. Tell me or do not tell me.

LILY (*Quickly, loudly*) Mama, we're rich.

ALBERTINE Who?

LILY Julian.

ALBERTINE When you say rich, do you mean *money* rich or spiritual rich, or moral rich or—

LILY You're teasing me. Money rich.

ALBERTINE Well, isn't that nice. Julian didn't lose the factory?

LILY Yes, he lost it. We got rich some other way. There were phone calls from a lady and Julian would talk so I couldn't understand, and then we came here, and it all has to do with the lady, I think, and something else—

ALBERTINE (*Very quickly*) Never mind. Never mind. He'll probably tell me. What good news, Lily. I must say I hadn't expected it. Forgive my bringing the check. How impertinent of me to take for granted that Julian needed it. Don't tell him, just tear it up. Tonight we'll have a celebration—if I still know how. Shall we dine at Galatoire's? (*When there is no answer, she stares at* LILY) What trouble are you in?

LILY First we lived in a big hotel in Chicago, and I didn't like it, and didn't have anything to do. Then we moved to a little, poor hotel and I learned to cook in the bathroom, and Julian and I were close together, and he didn't have his friends any more, and he was sad and sweet and often he stayed with me all day, in bed, and we'd read or sleep, and he'd tell me about things. We were never really hungry, but I'd have to watch the meat and give him my share when he wasn't looking because he likes meat, and I was very happy.

ALBERTINE How often the rich like to play at being poor. A rather nasty game, I've always thought. You had only to write me.

LILY It wasn't a game, it wasn't. It was just after he lost all his money in the factory—

ALBERTINE *Your* money in the factory. You like being poor and you're not going to be. Is that the trouble you are in? I can't be sorry for you, Lily. I don't think Julian would have liked the meat game for very long; and neither would you if the shortage had lasted much longer. (*Laughs*) Cheer up. Good fortune isn't as bad as it seems.

LILY You're laughing at me, and you shouldn't. Julian will leave me now.

ALBERTINE Why?

LILY He is different. Things have changed.

ALBERTINE Marriages change from day to day and year to year. All relations between people. Women, of course, have regrets for certain delicate early minutes, but— There is no answer to that.

LILY Did you, Mama? Did you have those regrets?

ALBERTINE I don't remember. I don't think so. Your father and I had very little together. And so we had little to regret.

LILY I don't mean my father.

ALBERTINE (*After a long silence*) I came here because you were in trouble, or so you said. Not because I am. When I come to you for that reason, feel free to say what you wish. Until then, please do not.

LILY Julian couldn't have me last night, and when I cried he said please not to, that— And so I went out and walked and walked. I had never seen that street before. I heard noise way up, and I went in. There were people and a woman stood before them on a box. The people talked about themselves right out loud. One woman had lost a leg but she said it was growing back and she proved it.

(*There is a long pause*)

ALBERTINE My. Are you dozing off?

LILY And a man stood up and said how he used to drink and use a gun. And the lady on the box kept saying, "Truth, truth is the way to life, and the one way, the only way. Open your hearts with this knife and throw them here." (*Throws up her arm*) She had a knife in her hand—

ALBERTINE Do sit down, Lily.

LILY And she kissed the knife—

(*She kisses her hand in imitation*)

ALBERTINE Strange tastes people have. Don't kiss your own hand again, please.

LILY (*Sits down, speaks quietly*) Everybody left and there I was. The woman said, "You want me, child?" And I said, "Could I buy your knife?" "No," she said. "The knife is not for sale." But I wanted it more than I ever wanted anything and, well—(*Smiles, slyly*)—finally, we swapped something— And when it was in my hand, for the first time in my life, I just said everything, and asked. The lady said the knife of truth would dress me as in a jacket of iron flowers and though I would do battle, I would march from the battle cleansed. Then I fell asleep—

ALBERTINE Your many religious experiences have always made me uneasy, Lily—

LILY When I woke up I knew that I must begin my struggle up the mountain path of truth by asking you—

ALBERTINE You telephoned at two this morning to speak with me about a journey up a mountain path of truth?

LILY And Henry came instead, and made me get in the car, and brought me *here*. He stood in the way— But he can't. Because I must ask truth, and speak truth, and act with truth, now and forever.

ALBERTINE Do you think this is the proper climate? So hot and damp. Puts mildew on the truth.

LILY Did you sell me to Julian, Mama?
(ALBERTINE *rises, comes to* LILY, *stares at her, and takes her by the shoulders*)

ALBERTINE (*Softly*) Lily, take hold of yourself. Take hold.

LILY Answer me.

ALBERTINE You are my child, but I will not take much more of this.

LILY (*In a cry*) Mama, Mama, I didn't mean to hurt you. (*Puts her hand on* ALBERTINE'S *chest*) But it's so bad for me. Julian may leave me now, and he's all I ever had, or will, or want—Mama, did he marry me for money?

ALBERTINE He married you because he loved you. Shame on you, Lily. You are looking for pain, and that makes me sad and always has.

LILY I told you there is another woman. I saw them. I followed them and they went places where people wouldn't see them and they talked. And she has something to do with his getting rich.

ALBERTINE Do you intend him never to speak to another woman? I don't know what you are talking about, getting rich, but it's good for people to have money of their own. The day comes when they don't like taking it from others. I know people thought of Julian as a charming man who didn't care about such things. But I never thought so.

LILY Last night when I lay waiting for him, and he knew it, he said he'd had too much champagne and he wanted to sleep alone. It's been like that since the lady came to Chicago.

ALBERTINE You've learned women's chitchat very fast. I'm not good at this, but since we've started I can tell you everybody wants to sleep alone sometimes—(*Laughs*)—maybe most of the time.

LILY He liked to come to bed with me. You didn't know that, did you?

ALBERTINE I have not read it in the newspaper. But, as you

know, I'm a large stockholder, and if you'd like it reported in detail—(*She breaks off, puts her hand over her eyes*) Forgive me.

LILY You'd never believed anybody could want me. I didn't believe it, either. I was so scared at first that I— But there I was, good for the man I loved. He said I was better than anybody, and that I must learn to cook because he'd always believed that a woman who was good in the bedroom was good in the kitchen—(*She laughs happily*) And I did learn. What do you think of that?

ALBERTINE I think well of it.

LILY (*Softly*) I was beloved, Mama, and I flourished. Now I'm frightened. Help me.

ALBERTINE (*Gently*) How can I help you when I don't understand what you're talking about? Are you really saying that if Julian stayed dependent on you, all would be safe, but if he has money for himself, and need not crawl to you—

LILY That's an ugly way to speak, Mama.

ALBERTINE On your struggle up the mountain path, you will find that truth is often ugly. It burns. (*After a second*) I don't believe there is any other woman, but in any case, be wise enough to wait and find out.

LILY I don't want to be wise, ever, Mama, ever. I'm in love.

ALBERTINE Then be happy that Julian has finally had a little luck. Lily, he would have come to hate your money. *That* was the danger I feared for you.

LILY I never wanted us to have money. I hate money. You know that, Mama.

ALBERTINE Then be very careful. Same thing as loving it.

*(The phone rings and* LILY *wheels and makes a dash for the house. At the same minute,* ANNA, *who has been moving in and out of the room, packing the valise, now turns from the valise and crosses to the phone.* LILY *falls over the porch steps and rolls to the ground.* HENRY *runs toward her)*

LILY Anna! Anna!

ALBERTINE Lily.

ANNA *(Into the phone)* I will wake him. Just a minute.

*(She moves out.* ALBERTINE *moves to help* LILY *rise)*

LILY *(Calling to* ANNA*)* That's the woman. I want to speak to her. I want to ask her—

*(She makes a sudden, violent movement up the porch steps)*

ALBERTINE No. *(Very sharply)* No.

*(*HENRY *touches* LILY*'s arm as if to keep her from moving)*

LILY *(To* HENRY*)* Leave me alone. I told you that last night. I told it to you years ago when I rolled down the hill. I meant to roll down the hill and kill myself, but you didn't know it.

HENRY I knew it.

*(*JULIAN *appears in the living room, dressed in a robe, the envelope of money in his pocket. He moves to the phone)*

JULIAN Hello. Sorry about the call last night. I was dying to tell you the good news, but of course I couldn't call you back. Did the cough medicine work? Did you have a good night's sleep? This is the great day, so stop worrying. Everything went fine. Got it right here in my pocket, nice clean bills. Eleven o'clock, waving a fortune at you. Where we agreed. (*He listens, smiling*) I did everything the way you told me, only better. Don't worry about me. He just beats women. (*Gently, affectionately*) I'll be there. Good-bye, my dear. (ANNA *enters the living room carrying a glass of juice and a dress.* JULIAN *takes the juice from* ANNA, *kisses her*) What's good for breakfast?

ANNA Pancakes?

JULIAN (*Looks around at the old dress she is packing*) Why are you taking all that old stuff? Throw out everything old. (*Stares at* ANNA) What's the matter with you. You look terrible.

ALBERTINE (*Through the window*) Morning, Julian.

(ANNA *exits toward the kitchen*)

JULIAN Well, look who's here. Hello. (*He starts out for the porch, stops, kicks aside a few packages, grabs a small one and runs out*) A present for you.

ALBERTINE Thank you.

(*He turns to* LILY)

JULIAN Hello, darling. (*Stares at her*) What's the matter with you? (LILY *shakes her head. He kisses her, and moves toward* ALBERTINE, *with whom he shakes hands. He sees* HENRY *and they shake hands*) How's the fishing? Been up the bayou?

HENRY Been up. But nobody got anything. Except crayfish.

JULIAN Anybody asked what I missed most in Chicago, I'd have said a bayou, a bowl of crayfish, a good gun for a flight of wild ducks coming over— Going to buy a little place up there, first thing. You're welcome all the time. (*Sees that* LILY *has not moved and is staring at the ground*) What's the matter, Lily? (*When she doesn't answer, he speaks to* ALBERTINE) I sure manage to depress my ladies. Never used to be that way. Do I depress you?

ALBERTINE (*Laughs*) I'm very glad to see you.

(*She has now unwrapped the package and taken out a flame-red lace mantilla supported by a giant comb. She arranges it on her head*)

JULIAN What's it meant for?

ALBERTINE I don't know.

JULIAN When do you wear it?

ALBERTINE I'll wear it for reading in bed. How very nice of you to bring it to me.

JULIAN (*As if the tone of thanks puzzles him*) How nice of *you*. You put it on. Nobody else—(*Turns to* LILY) Lily, did you show your mama your new ring? (LILY *shakes her head*) Oh. Go and get your ring and show your mama. (LILY *hesitates and then moves inside. He smiles ruefully at* ALBERTINE, *points to the mantilla*) Silly present, isn't it? It cost a lot.

ALBERTINE (*Laughs*) Nice to buy, nice to get, silly presents. Who wants a roast of beef?

(*She removes the mantilla and carefully folds it*)

JULIAN (*Smiles with pleasure*) That's what I thought— (*Confidentially, points inside*) I think I bought, got, brought— Well, they're sort of upset and they don't think I know it. I should have had sense enough to know that when you've been poor and wanted things you couldn't have, your stomach gets small and you can't eat much right away. I brought too much, and everything too grand, and, well. Guess they got a little sick. They're so happy that it comes out unhappy. You know how it is?

ALBERTINE I don't think so.

JULIAN It's a crazy old world. For years, they—(*Points inside*)—tell me about what's going to be, what I'm going to do, you know, get rich and big time. The more I fail, the louder they cheer me with what we're all going to have, want. And so all my life I dream about coming up those steps carrying everything, and I make up what they will say, and what I will say—(*Smiles*) Well, when it came, I guess it was hard to believe, maybe even frightened them, I never thought of that, and I just bought anything if it cost a lot, and made Carrie sick on caviar, and everybody acted scared, and like they were going to cry. Lily did cry— Natural enough. You know?

ALBERTINE (*Carefully*) No, I don't know. You've had good fortune and brought it home. There's something sad in not liking what you want when you get it. And something strange, maybe even mean. (*Sharply, as if in warning*) Nobody should have cried about your good fortune, nobody should have been anything but happy.

JULIAN No, no. You don't understand. They're happy. They just haven't had time— I scared them, Europe and a house and fancy things all in a day. Who wouldn't be scared? They thought I'd come home broke— God knows I always had— You don't know about that, but *they* do, and they got ready to give me all they had, and tell all the same nice lies about how the next time. And then there I come, strutting like a kid—(*Laughs with great pleasure*) Rich. Rich. Rich. (*As a child would say it*) I'm as good as you now. Isn't that true?

ALBERTINE (*Laughs*) I'm not sure.

JULIAN We'll have to have long talks and consultations.

ALBERTINE About money? I don't think so. I like it very much. But it makes dull talk.

JULIAN Oh, I just bet you don't really think that. (*He pokes her with his finger; she stares at him and sits very straight*) That's just the way *you* people want *us* to think. Not dull at all. Why, I had more fun this week— Know what I did?

(*He pokes her again. She reacts sharply and* HENRY *laughs. She turns to look at* HENRY *and then turns back to* JULIAN, *smiling*)

ALBERTINE Henry doesn't like people to poke me, do you, Henry?

HENRY I never saw anybody do it before.

JULIAN I went to see a man I hated the two times I ever saw him and the many times I heard about him. Once when he teased me as a boy, and once when he made fun of me as a man. (*He stops, remembers, sighs*) I guess he's the only man

I ever hated. Well, I went right in his office and said I got something you want, and I'll take a hundred and fifty thousand dollars for it. After he said all about being crazy, and to get the hell out, he said, "Get your money from women—your sisters or your wife. You married her for it"—(JULIAN *rises, speaks softly to* ALBERTINE) Did people think that? Did they?

ALBERTINE I don't see people. I never thought it.

JULIAN (*Leans down, kisses her hand*) Maybe I'll knock you down later, I said to him, but right now let's keep our minds on a hundred and fifty thousand dollars delivered a week from today. (*To* ALBERTINE) Want to see?

(*He takes the envelope from his pocket and holds it open for her*)

ALBERTINE (*Laughs*) It does look nice. I don't think I ever saw anything larger than a hundred-dollar bill.

JULIAN I tell you, the rich don't have any fun with money.

ALBERTINE Smells rather nice, too.

JULIAN I put a little cologne water on it. (*As he puts the envelope back in his pocket*) One hundred and fifty thousand dollars. Do people like you think it's a lot of money?

ALBERTINE It's money. (*Very deliberately pokes him*) People like me think it's a good beginning. It's not a great fortune, but if you want one it will start you off.

JULIAN You know, I think so, too. (*Smiles at her*) Isn't it funny? I liked you, but I never talked easy with you before. Now you just seem to me like anybody else.

ALBERTINE I'm sorry.

JULIAN (*Leans over and kisses her cheek*) I didn't mean it quite like that. I just mean that you always scared me, and now you don't. I guess most people like you scared me. (*Smiles*) I was kind of, well, kind of broken. I knew it, but I showed off to keep—(*He points inside*)—them from—(*He turns to* HENRY) It's bad for a man to feel gone. (*Then, very gaily*) Like a miracle. I go in to see this bastard shaking, and I come out knowing I did fine, knowing I'm going to be all right forever. You understand it wasn't just the money?

ALBERTINE (*Laughs*) I don't understand very much. Why don't you wait and tell me when you can?

JULIAN All I mean, you do something right. *Just right.* You know a man's got to have what you've got—very different from trying to get a job or selling something he don't want. I just sat there calm and smiling until he got through trying to find out how I, *I,* bought two acres of swamp land before he did, and how I could know how much he needed it. I thought to myself, so this is the way the big boys do it, you poor fool for being so scared all your life. So I said, "Get through, will you, I got a board of directors meeting and have no more time for you." (*Laughs with pleasure*) I don't know where I got that from. Maybe the movies. You and my lawyer can attend to the rest, so agree or don't agree, I don't want to be in the room with you too long. He got white but he didn't say anything, so I got up and started out and he said, "All right. Give us two weeks to draw the papers"— My lawyer said, "Fair enough, sir," and I guess it was the "sir" that made me angry because I said, "No. I'll take it next Tuesday at two o'clock. Have it ready." And I walked out the happiest man in town. I paid back my life some way or other—(GUS *appears carrying ice*) You can lose for just so long— When you win, everything on you grows bigger, know what I mean?

(*He laughs and pokes* ALBERTINE)

ALBERTINE And I grow black and blue.

GUS Hi. Home to stay?

JULIAN Gus, just look at that new icebox. (GUS *turns, stares in through the porch door*) Bought it more for you than for them.

GUS In Chicago they keep it in the parlor?

JULIAN Gus, my old friend Gus. You're going to have that farm, kid. Go find it and start with this.

(*He hands* GUS *several large bills.* GUS *looks at them, but doesn't take them*)

GUS You at that again?

JULIAN This time I made it. Throw the ice away—(*He shoves the money into* GUS' *hand*)

GUS Julian, I don't want that kind of trouble again.

JULIAN Nobody'll come for it this time. I'm telling you the truth. And there's as much more as you want. Now get going and find the farm.

GUS Who the hell wants a farm? Got enough trouble. Where'd you make up the farm from?

(*He goes around the garden and disappears*)

JULIAN He said since we were kids about a farm— People talk about what they want, and then— How's that?

ALBERTINE I guess most of us make up things we want, don't get them, and get too old, or too lazy, to make up new ones. Best not to disturb that, Julian. People don't want other people to guess they never knew what they wanted in the first place.

JULIAN That's real sad. I know what I want and *I'm* going to be happy getting it.

ALBERTINE Well, I like nice, rich, happy relatives, although I never had any. But I have bad news for you, Julian—it's not simple being happy, and money doesn't seem to have much to do with it, although it has to do with other things more serious.

(CARRIE *comes in, moving slowly. She stops when she sees the group*)

JULIAN Morning. Where you been?

CARRIE I—I've been downtown.

JULIAN Buying things, I hope. (*To* ALBERTINE) My sisters are going to Europe tomorrow. Isn't that fine, after years of—

CARRIE Your sisters are not—(*Then, softly*) come inside, please.

JULIAN What's the matter?

CARRIE (*Starts toward the steps, sharply*) Come inside.

JULIAN (*Playfully, but with meaning*) Carrie, stop talking like that. You got a new man on your hands. You got to talk to me different now, like I'm a tycoon. (*To* ALBERTINE) What's a tycoon? How much, I mean?

ALBERTINE Miss Carrie can tell you. She works for one.

JULIAN Barrett? Is he? I don't want to be like Barrett—

CARRIE He knows what you think of him. He'd already read your letter when I got there. I can't tell you what I felt. All I could think to say was that it was a joke and you'd be down later to apologize.

JULIAN (*After a second*) Did you? Did you really say that? Don't ever say that again, Carrie. That's one of things I don't ever have to do any more. That's one of things money's going to buy us all.

CARRIE I want to see you alone, Julian.

JULIAN I don't think you should have gone to see him at all. We'll talk about it another time. I'm busy today. (*She wheels around, angry.* JULIAN *is grinning at* ALBERTINE) How you like me? See? Got no time for small matters.

CARRIE Small matters? After nineteen years. He said he didn't believe you wrote the letter. He said I wrote it, that it was like me, that he always had known about—(*She gasps*)—things in me. After nineteen years of loyalty— I want you to get dressed and go tell him that if you owe him an apology, he owes me an apology for the awful words he said—

JULIAN (*To* ALBERTINE) That's how tycoons act toward loyal ladies?

ALBERTINE I don't know how they act toward loyal ladies.

CARRIE Julian—

ALBERTINE I do know tycoons are not romantic about money and the happiness it buys.

JULIAN Ah, can't I be romantic for a month?

(CARRIE *moves into the living room and stands waiting*)

ALBERTINE All right. We'll give you a month. After a month I suggest venality. You'll find more people understand it and are less suspicious of it. Right now it's my impression that everyone around here thinks you held up a bank.

JULIAN No, a poker game. Or a jewel robbery. Hey, Lily. Lily! Come and show your mama your ring. Lily! (*To* ALBERTINE) *You* don't think I stole the money, do you?

(*He looks at his watch, then moves quickly toward the porch as* LILY *appears*)

ALBERTINE (*Because* JULIAN *is going up the steps of the porch, and because she speaks very softly, he does not hear her*) No. I think I know where you got it.

JULIAN (*As he passes* LILY, *he picks up her left hand*) Go show your mama— Where's your ring?

LILY Somewhere.

JULIAN Where is somewhere?

LILY Don't be angry, please—

JULIAN Why not? (*He moves into the room, sees* CARRIE, *smiles*) Seen a large diamond ring?

CARRIE Up to yesterday we never had such problems. How does one look for a diamond ring? Julian, he said bad things to me. Julian. (*He doesn't answer, and starts to leave the room*) Julian. Please answer me.

JULIAN Answer you what?

CARRIE Once, and not long ago, you'd have known by my face, and you'd have kissed me and said, "What is it, my Carrie?"
(*Behind* CARRIE, ANNA *appears carrying a breakfast tray. She stops*)

JULIAN (*Gently*) What is it, my Carrie?

CARRIE I want to talk to you— Let's go by ourselves, the way we used to—

JULIAN I'm due downtown—

CARRIE You have no time for me. We're coming apart, you and I—

JULIAN What are you talking about?

CARRIE You've come home in all this mystery, and not said a word with me alone—

JULIAN When I take you to the boat tomorrow, I'll tell you all about "this mystery"—

CARRIE I want to speak to you now. Now.

JULIAN (*Softly*) Did you always use that tone with me? Did you? (*To* ANNA) Did you? (*When she doesn't answer*) Say something, so I can tell the way you talk to me.

ANNA Breakfast.

JULIAN (*Takes the tray from her*) Will you press a shirt for me?

(*She nods and moves off with him*)

CARRIE You're saying no to me, when I need you?

JULIAN I'm not saying no to you. I'm saying that I'm busy.

(*He sings as he exits*)

ALBERTINE (*To* LILY, *who is on the porch*) What did you do with the ring?

LILY I don't want it.

ALBERTINE He will be hurt. I suggest that you pretend that you do want it.

LILY I don't want it.

(CARRIE, *nervously moving about, comes to stand at the window and to listen to the voices in the garden*)

ALBERTINE There are many ways of loving. I'm sure yours must be among them. Put white flowers in your hair, walk up your mountain path of truth with a white banner in your hand and as you drop it on his head, speak of love.

LILY I gave her the ring and she gave me the knife.

ALBERTINE I beg your pardon?

HENRY (*Quickly*) I know what she means.

LILY I gave the lady the ring and she gave me the knife. I didn't want the ring, and I didn't know Julian would care. But I will go and tell him the truth now and—

(*She starts into the room*)

ALBERTINE You asked my advice and here it is: You do too much. Go and do nothing for a while. Nothing. I have seen you like this before. (*With force*) I tell you now, do nothing. (*To* HENRY) You know the address of the upstairs knife lady?

LILY Mama, don't make fun of her—

ALBERTINE No, indeed. We will try to find your ring. Decide whether your costume is meant for day or night, and rest yourself. (*Softly*) Lily, don't tell Julian about the ring. (LILY *nods and enters the house. She sees* CARRIE, *smiles at her, and exits toward the kitchen.* ANNA *appears carrying a shirt and crosses the room toward the kitchen*) Well, there it is.

HENRY You are not wise with Lily.

ALBERTINE No. I never was. Well, it's been a good year, hasn't it? The best I ever had.

HENRY Nothing has happened.

ALBERTINE I know Lily. You do, too.

HENRY She is jealous and scared—

ALBERTINE And nothing I say will stop her from being foolish. And of course there is another woman. But Julian isn't sleeping with her. (*Laughs*) They raised him to be a very, very moral man.

HENRY Very, very moral men sometimes sleep with women. I think.

ALBERTINE But it shows on them. Do you think he's sleeping with another woman?

HENRY He's not sleeping with her, and he won't. But he used to.

ALBERTINE Yes? (*When there is no answer*) Cy Warkins is the man he's talking about, Cy Warkins who bought what he calls his two acres of swamp land. I'm not sure why Cy wanted it so much, but if it's down by the river I can make a good guess. Warkins owns fifty percent of the stock of the interstate agreement to take the railroad route along the docks. (*Laughs*) If my guess is right, he must have been surprised that Julian knew about the best kept secret in years. I regret not being there when Julian told him. But who told Julian?

Mrs. Warkins? (HENRY *does not answer*) She never liked Warkins and that was the only thing I ever knew about her. But she must be forty now. (*When there is no answer*) But of course she wasn't always forty. (*She points inside*) They knew each other? And she told him about the railroad? I'm not gossiping, you know that.

HENRY I think that's what happened. She was in love with Julian once. She hates Warkins and has wanted to leave for years. Maybe this is the money to leave with.

ALBERTINE (*Softly, in a new tone, as if it is forced out of her, and she is ashamed*) How do you know about Mrs. Warkins? Please.

HENRY I don't know about her any more, but I used to. She's a cousin to me.

ALBERTINE (*Stares at him, and then laughs*) She's part colored? Isn't that wonderful! Did Warkins know when he married her?

HENRY He doesn't know now. But Julian did, and didn't care. She's a foolish woman and grateful for such things.

ALBERTINE That's understandable, God knows.

HENRY Not to me. I am not grateful, nor ungrateful, nor any word like that.

ALBERTINE Nor should you be. You are in a bad humor with me this morning. You are disapproving. What have I done or said?

HENRY (*Softly*) You look tired.

ALBERTINE (*Rises, goes to him*) The world has many people who make things too hard for too little reason, or none at all, or the pleasure, or stupidity. We've never done that, you and I.

HENRY Yes, we've done it. But we've tried not to.

(ALBERTINE *touches his hand.* HENRY *smiles and puts her hand to his face.* ALBERTINE *turns and, as she does, she sees* CARRIE *in the window.* ALBERTINE *pauses, turns slightly to where* CARRIE *has been sitting as if to ask herself what* CARRIE *could have heard*)

ALBERTINE Are you writing a book, Miss Carrie?

CARRIE (*Softly*) This is our house, Mrs. Prine.

ALBERTINE (*Sighs*) Indeed.

(HENRY *takes her arm and they move off.* LILY *comes running into the room, holding her right hand in her left hand. She is followed by* ANNA, *who carries a bottle and gauze bandage.* LILY *runs toward the hall, calling out*)

LILY Julian, I—I cut my hand.

ANNA Lily.

LILY Julian. I cut my hand. (*Then she turns and calls out loudly toward the garden*) Mama. Mama. I cut my hand.

CARRIE Your mama has left with her friend.

(JULIAN *appears, rubbing his wet hair with a bath towel*)

JULIAN What's the matter?

LILY I cut my hand.

JULIAN (*He picks up* LILY's *hand, holds it for* ANNA *to bandage*) It's a deep one. You ought not to have rusty knives in the kitchen.

(ANNA *looks up as if she is about to speak, but changes her mind*)

LILY Ouch. (*She turns her hand toward* JULIAN. *He kisses it and she gently touches his face. She rubs her thigh*) And last night I fell in here and hit my leg. You could cure that, too. Please. Make me cured, Julian. Let's go to bed and maybe you'll be pleased with me— Maybe. (*She puts his hand on her breast.* ANNA *turns away;* CARRIE *stands staring at them*) And if you're pleased with me, then all the bad will go away, and I will pray for it to be that way. But if you're not, I'll understand, and won't ask why—(*She laughs gaily, slyly, and presses his hand on her breast*) But *if* you are pleased with me, darling— (JULIAN *leans down to kiss her*) I have missed you.

(*He picks her up in his arms and begins to move out of the room*)

CARRIE (*Sucks in her breath; loudly*) I read in a French book that there was nothing so abandoned as a respectable young girl.

JULIAN (*Laughs*) That's true, thank God. (*He leans down to kiss* LILY's *hair*) Otherwise nobody could stand them.

(LILY *laughs merrily*)

CARRIE (*Comes toward them*) You didn't fall in here last night. When I turned on the light—

LILY Yes, ma'am. I fell. I didn't see the spinet—
(JULIAN, *carrying* LILY, *exits*)

CARRIE You did not fall against the spinet. You were on this side of the room, hitting—

ANNA Carrie.

CARRIE She was hitting herself against that table. Just doing it. I saw her. I tell you, I saw her.

ANNA I believe you.

CARRIE He doesn't know she went out last night. He doesn't know she gave her ring away—to some woman— She's told him lies. She lies to him, she tricks him. I think she's a crazy girl—(*Points to the garden*) And that woman knows it. I think there's a crazy girl in there—

ANNA (*Softly, as if to herself*) She cut her hand, quite deliberately and calmly, with a knife she took from a valise. She said a kind of prayer over the knife—

CARRIE (*Moves swiftly toward* ANNA) You saw her do that? You saw her cut herself? I tell you she's crazy.
(*She moves toward the door, right*)

ANNA No.

CARRIE How can you stand what's happening here? He comes

home with all this money nonsense. He's married to a crazy girl. I think he's in bed with a girl—

ANNA —he wanted. It's not our business.

CARRIE It is our business that our brother sells something to Mr. Cyrus Warkins for a fortune Mr. Cyrus Warkins doesn't wan't to pay. Warkins is a powerful and dangerous man in this town, and Julian would be a baby in the hands of such a man—

ANNA What are you talking about?

CARRIE I don't know all it means. (*Points out to the garden*) But I heard them say this money, or whatever, has to do with Warkins' wife.

ANNA He slept with Charlotte Warkins ten years ago. It's been over that long.

CARRIE How do you know such a thing? How do *you* know?

ANNA Because he told me.

CARRIE I don't believe you. You're a liar.

ANNA Be quiet, Carrie.

CARRIE You've made it up, you always made up things like that. It didn't happen. He was an innocent boy—(ANNA *laughs.* CARRIE *unbuttons the neck of her dress as if she were choking*) He would never have told *you*. He would have told me. He was closer to me— There he is, another man, not our brother, lost to us after all the years of work and care, married to a crazy little whore who cuts her hand to try to get him into bed—(*Points to the garden*) The daughter of a woman who keeps a nigger fancy man. I'll bet she paid Julian to take that crazy girl away from her—

ANNA Stop that talk. You know that's not true. Stop talking about Julian that way.

CARRIE Let's go and ask him. Let's go and ask your darling child. Your favorite child, the child you made me work for, the child I lost my youth for— You used to tell us that when you love, truly love, you take your chances on being hated by speaking out the truth. (*Points inside*) Go in and do it.

ANNA All right. I'll take that chance now and tell you that you want to sleep with him and always have. Years ago I used to be frightened that you would try and I would watch you and suffer for you.

CARRIE (*After a second, in a whisper*) You never said those words. Tell me I never heard those words. Tell me, Anna. (*When there is no answer*) You were all I ever had. I don't love you any more.

ANNA That was the chance I took.

*Curtain*

# ACT THREE

## ACT THREE

CARRIE *is as she was.* ANNA's *suitcases are on the porch. She enters, puts another suitcase below the piano, and exits. Offstage, there is a loud whistling, from* JULIAN. CARRIE *crosses to the spinet and begins to pick out the melody he is whistling. He enters, dressed except for his shirt, and carrying his coat. He is singing and he smiles pleasantly at* CARRIE.

JULIAN (*Singing*)

This is the big day, this is the great day
This is the Berniers day.
Never been one, no, never never,
Never been such a Berniers day.
Never been such a day before.
Going to be more and plenty more.
Oh, it's money day, the end of trouble day,
And going to be more and plenty more.
Never been such a day before.
Not for Mama, not for Papa,
Not for Sister, not for Brother—
Going to be more and plenty more.
(*Shouts off*) Anna! Where's my shirt?

CARRIE (*Softly*) Do you know that all I want in this world is what will be good for you?

JULIAN And I for you (ANNA *appears carrying his shirt. He crosses to take it from her, puts it on, and sings to* ANNA)

Now every day she going to be
She going to be a Berniers day.
Say every day she going to be
She going to be a Berniers day,
And for Mama and for Papa
And for Sister and for Brother
Going to be just a Berniers day.

(*To* ANNA)

It's the best day of my life since I won the bag of marbles from old Gus. You made me give them back. You said he was a poor colored boy. But I was a poor white boy so I didn't know what you were getting so fancy about. Well, I'm on my way to the best day. (*To* CARRIE, *pointing to valise*) Getting packed? Getting excited?

CARRIE (*Pats the spinet*) I'll practice today and tonight I'll give a little concert for you and we'll sing all the pieces you used to like.

(ANNA *begins to move out of the room*)

JULIAN Er. We'll be leaving today. (ANNA *stops, turns.* CARRIE *rises*) We'll be going. (*Nervously*) And *you'll* be leaving tomorrow, so just one day. 'Course I'll wait until tomorrow if you need me—

CARRIE Where are you going?

JULIAN Maybe a camping trip, maybe New York—

CARRIE A few weeks?

JULIAN I don't know. No. A year or so. And then back here, of course. This is where I belong. Where I want to be, where

I was meant to be. (*Overcheerful*) And by that time you world travelers will be back and—

CARRIE *You* want to go? Or *Lily* wants to go?

JULIAN Never seen New York, either of us.

CARRIE Lily wants to go.

JULIAN I don't know. I just decided. We'll come back, don't worry, and—(*He crosses to the chest and takes out savings bankbook*)

CARRIE Why did you suddenly decide to go? Why?

JULIAN (*Holds up the bankbook*) Some people got a family Bible. We got a savings bankbook. (*Softly, to* CARRIE) Don't look like that. (*Points inside*) She's young and— I don't think she wanted to come back. I didn't think about it before but— And maybe we should be alone for a while. That's all. (*Points to the bankbook.*) Twenty thousand going in here this morning. Twenty thousand dollars. That going to be enough? (*Laughs with pleasure*) For six months maybe? Enough?

ANNA I don't know anything about twenty thousand dollars.

JULIAN You got to learn fast. Fast, I say. What was the word Mama used to use?

CARRIE (*In a cry*) Julian, don't go—

ANNA (*Very fast*) *Faner. Elle commence a se faner.* The leaf came in the spring, stayed nice on the branch in the autumn until the winter winds would blow it in the snow. Mama said that in that little time of holding on, a woman had to make ready for the winter ground where she would lie the rest of her life. A leaf cannot rise from the ground and go back to the tree, remember that. I remembered it. But when it came there was nothing I could do.

JULIAN (*Gently, touches her*) Mama was mean.

CARRIE (*Shrilly*) Anna always says something about Mama when things are wrong. Always. Mama wasn't mean to you. Just to us.

JULIAN Did you think I liked it that way? Did you? Mama had a tough time, I guess. That often makes people mean. (*Softly, to* ANNA) You're still on the tree, still so nice and pretty, and when the wind does come, a long time from now, I'll be there to catch you with a blanket made of warm roses, and a parasol of dollar bills to keep off the snow. Dollar bills make a mighty nice parasol, I just bet you. (*Smiles*) For another good lady, too. (*As if to himself*) Well, I'm off to give them to her. I'll walk right down Sailor's Lane and she'll be waiting for me. I'll take her arm, we'll have a cup of coffee, and I'll try to say thank you. No, I won't. People are always saying thank you so they can forget what they said it for. (*Holds up one envelope*) I'll just hand this to her and say, "Have a good life, baby," and then I'll walk her down to the depot and put her on the train. A happy day. (*Holds up other envelope*) Then I'll go around and bank our share. That'll make me respectable, won't it?

ANNA (*After a second*) Is she *fanée?*

JULIAN Yes. A long time ago.

ANNA Then wish her well from me.

JULIAN I will.

CARRIE Is the lady going to New York?

JULIAN I don't know where she's going. I guess so. Doesn't everybody go to New York? (LILY, *on the last of* CARRIE'S *speech, comes into the room.* JULIAN *turns and grins at her*) Want to go to New York, or a fishing trip to Canada, or the Grand Canyon, or— Today?

LILY With you?

JULIAN (*Crosses to her, holds her face with his hand*) How would you like that? Time we found a place. Wherever.

LILY You and me?

JULIAN You and me.

LILY In a room?

JULIAN (*Laughs*) In a room, or a boat, or a tent—

LILY Just you and me. And will the not happening, happen to us again?

JULIAN (*Sharply*) Lily, stop that. I was tired and I had too much to drink last night. And I was nervous the last few days and am now. Any man will tell you that happens. (*Then, smiling*) Only you must never talk such things with any man, hear me?

LILY (*Giggles*) I won't.

(*She drops the knife from her right hand. She looks down at it as if surprised*)

JULIAN (*Leans down, picks up the knife, stares at it*) What in the name of God is this?

LILY The knife of truth. Will you swear on it? Swear that you will keep me with you whatever—

JULIAN For Christ's sake, Lily. What the hell's the matter with you? (*He drops the knife on the table*) Stop talking foolish and stop playing with knives. Maybe kiddies should marry kiddies. But I'm thirty-four. Stop talking about last night and what didn't happen, because it's the kind of thing you don't talk about. Can't you understand that? (*Gently*) Now go pack your bags and go tell your mama we're going away.

LILY (*Laughing with pleasure*) Can I say we're going away forever? Just us.

JULIAN Forever. Just us. (*Turns, sees* CARRIE *and* ANNA, *and stops*) I mean we'll come back here, or the folks will come to us—(*Very fast*) You'll see. You'll come to visit us, we'll come to visit you— Buy us a little house up the bayou. Sometimes I wish I had gone on up the bayou years ago—

ANNA You did.

JULIAN Maybe I should have stayed. They said I was better with a muskrat boat than any Cajun, better with a gun. A nice little shack and a muskrat boat, all the bobwhite you could ever want— (*After a second*) Fine morning to be talking like this.

ANNA (*Sharply*) Go on.

LILY (*She runs toward* JULIAN, *holds him; he puts his arms around her*) Will you be coming back for me?

JULIAN What? What are you talking about? Lily, for Christ's sake. (*He kisses her, moves away; stops, looks pleadingly at all of them*) What's the matter? Please. It's the best day of my life. Please somebody look happy.

ANNA Go on. (*He smiles, moves out at a run.* LILY *follows him to the porch. He turns and kisses her and runs off. After a second,* LILY *sits down on the porch, as though she is very tired.* ANNA *speaks to* CARRIE) I wanted to be around the children he will have. I wanted something nice to grow old for. I held on to that and prayed for it. (*Very softly*) This time he will go forever.

CARRIE I don't believe it. You must have your headaches again. He will not go forever, or even for long—

ANNA This time I say he will go forever. You lusted and it showed. He doesn't know he saw it, but he did see it, and some day he'll know what he saw. (*With great violence*) You know the way that happens? You understand something, and don't know that you do, and forget about it. But one night years ago I woke up and knew what I had seen in you, and always seen. It will happen that way with him. It has already begun.

CARRIE I told you I didn't love you any more. Now I tell you that I hate you. We will have to find a way to live with that.

ANNA I don't think so.
(*She moves out to the porch on her way to the garden*)

LILY Will he come back for me, Miss Anna?

ANNA What's the matter with you, child? You must go and dress and pack your things. Julian won't be long and he'll want you to be ready. Shall I call your mother?

LILY She talked cold to me. (*She imitates her mother*) "Try not to excite yourself, Lily. Try to make yourself clear, Lily." But when she talks to Henry— (*In another voice; soft and gentle*) "Lily has gone to bed. Sit down. What shall we read tonight?" (*In her own voice*) And one night she said to him, "Oh, God, make the time when we can be alone; make it come before we are both too old to have pleasure from peace." (*Softly*) She would have paid anything for that time. Did she? Did she pay Julian? Is that why he took me?

ANNA (*Very sharply*) How dare you speak that way of Julian? What a bitter thought about a man who loves you.

LILY No. Who would want me for any other reason?

ANNA (*As she moves away*) Your modesty does not excuse you.

LILY I love him, Miss Anna. If he said he loved somebody else — Well, I'd just go away and he'd be rid of me. But this way— I know you understand.

ANNA A woman who marries a man she loves should have a little more happiness from it and talk a little more sense. That's all I understand.

LILY I've upset you, Miss Anna.

ANNA Yes. You're rather an expert.
(*She disappears around the garden.* CARRIE *has been sweeping the living room. She now moves to sweep the porch*)

LILY Cleaning day? (CARRIE *does not answer*) Do you like to sweep? I like to mop.

CARRIE Have you done much? Twice, say?

LILY I'm sorry you don't like me. I wanted you to.

CARRIE (*Gestures inside*) I would like to sweep the porch. Would you—

LILY Last night, in bed, Julian was thinking, I watched him. And thinking isn't the way to make love.

CARRIE I don't know much about gentlemen in bed and I don't want to learn from you.

LILY Haven't you ever slept with a man?
(CARRIE *turns and stares at* LILY)

CARRIE Shall we have a pillow fight or make fudge? I don't like these girlish confidences.

LILY I only thought you might like to know he was thinking of you, although, of course, I can't be sure. And maybe of Miss Anna, but most probably not.

CARRIE You'll be leaving here in an hour. Be satisfied with that victory and don't trust me with your dreams.

LILY Oh, Miss Carrie. I wanted you to like me.

CARRIE There is no need to worry about me any more.

LILY Oh, I do. And I will. I'm frightened of you.

CARRIE (*Angrily*) Your favorite word. Did it ever occur to you that other people are frightened, too?

LILY You? No. No, indeed. Of what, Miss Carrie?

CARRIE Of my hair which isn't nice any more, of my job which isn't there any more, of praying for small things and knowing just how small they are, of walking by a mirror when I didn't know it would be there—(*She gasps*) People say "Those Berniers girls, so devoted. That Carrie was pretty, and then one day she wasn't; just an old maid, working for her brother." They are right. An old maid with candied oranges as a right proper treat each Saturday night. We didn't see people any more, I guess, because we were frightened of saying or hearing more than we could stand. (*Very angrily*) There are lives that are shut and should stay shut, you hear me, and people who should not talk about themselves, and that was us.

LILY Why don't you come away with us, Miss Carrie?

CARRIE Stop sticking your baby pins into me. Go inside and pray that another woman won't do it to you. I want to clean the porch.

LILY There is another woman. I've seen her. Nobody believes me.

CARRIE I believe you.

LILY I don't know who she is. Do you?

CARRIE Your mother knows. Ask her.

LILY (*Giggles*) I just bet that's true. But Mama won't tell me because she doesn't like me and doesn't tell me things. (*Runs to* CARRIE) You know what does the harm? I keep thinking that Mama paid Julian to marry me. And then sometimes I think that's not true; he does love me. God made him love me because God knew how much I needed him. (*Smiles; ingratiating*) He just worships you, Miss Carrie, and I know he confides in you. Did he ever tell you Mama paid him? (*Grabs* CARRIE'*s arm and, in the force of the movement, throws* CARRIE *off balance*) Tell me. Be good to me. Tell me.

CARRIE (*Pulls away*) I tell you what I think: You're going to drive him crazy. (*She starts to move off.* LILY *grabs her*)

LILY Did my Mama—

CARRIE (*Angry*) I don't know what she did. All he told us was that he had fallen in love and was going to be married.

LILY (*In a transport of pleasure*) Oh. (*Laughing with happiness*) Miss Carrie; Miss Carrie! (*She pirouettes*) He told you he was in love! Isn't that nice?

CARRIE I remember wondering why he had picked that Sunday to tell us. Anna was going to the hospital the next morning for her eye operation. None of us had ever been in a hospital before, and we didn't know about the costs, and being in a ward, and all of that. So Julian came home and told about you, and then he said that Anna was going to have the best room in the hospital and he had called the great Dr. Kranz in Philadelphia, and the great Dr. Kranz was already on the train. He wouldn't let Anna say a word, said he won the money in a poker game. I don't know— Anna was more worried about that than about her eyes. And she fussed and fussed and never liked the fancy room and the uppity private nurses. But Dr. Kranz did a wonderful operation and when she came out of it, the first thing she said to Julian was, "My eyes were not made to make all this trouble for you." And he said a beautiful thing to her, he said, "Look, I'd give my both arms and one leg for you, but not two legs, so maybe I don't love you as much as I think," and how we all laughed. (*She smiles at* LILY) A few days later he brought you to see Anna. Do you remember?

LILY (*Who has been staring at* CARRIE) Yes.

CARRIE I was happy that Julian was to be married.

LILY You said so. (*Very loudly, as if out of control*) I didn't believe you.

CARRIE Oh, I could have stopped the marriage, even you must have guessed that.

LILY Even I. But you didn't stop it because you knew my mother had paid Julian—I'm glad I helped Miss Anna, I really am—would go on paying him, and you didn't have to worry about a little girl who didn't mean anything more to anybody than a bank check.

CARRIE I have said none of that: You have been looking for it, and you would have found it in anything I, or anybody else, could say.

LILY I don't mind, not much. It's better to know. I will take Julian any way I can have him. *If* I can have him. I feel most bad and sad, Miss Carrie, because what he married me for, he doesn't need any more. Isn't that true?

CARRIE I don't know. Take your questions to Mrs. Cyrus Warkins. She'll be in New York. You can have many a cozy evening.

LILY She's coming with us?

CARRIE No. She's going on the morning train.

LILY I see. Is she a tall, dark lady?

CARRIE I've never seen her. But Henry is tall and dark and she's his cousin, so perhaps. Your mother was very amused that the great lawyer Warkins had married a part nigger and didn't know it.

LILY Does Julian love her?

CARRIE I used to think I knew about Julian. I didn't. Ask your mother and her fancy man. They said Julian and the woman were together years ago. And my sister confirms the alliance.

LILY (*Giggles too loudly*) Together? Alliance? Together in bed? Alliance in bed? What a funny way to say it. Julian told me that you talked like an old maid when you were twelve years old, and that Gus used to say you kept your vagina in the icebox, that he'd seen it there and shut the door fast.

CARRIE (*Very loudly*) Stop that filthy talk. Julian never said a thing like that—

LILY Oh, please, I didn't mean to offend you. Julian said it in fun. Afterwards in bed, we always talked fun. That's almost the best time, when you laugh and say things you'd never say anyplace else, and it's all in honor bright. It's then that you ask about other girls, everybody does Julian told me, and every man thinks it's a big bore he's got to get through for the next time, if you know what I mean. Julian said there was only one woman that ever mattered, long ago, and I wasn't to worry—(*She laughs*)—and that she was married to a bastard who beat her, and if he ever made money he'd give it to her to get away. (*She smiles*) So now she's coming with us. What will they do with me? (*She screams*) It pains me. I can't tell you. I'll ask her not to come. (*She turns and runs up the porch and into the room, toward the phone*) I'll tell her I don't blame her, of course, and I'll swear on my knife of truth that if I have just one more year—(*Grabs the phone book, drops it, holds it out to* CARRIE) Please find it for me.

CARRIE Mrs. Warkins isn't home. She's waiting for Julian.

LILY (*Runs toward the porch*) I'll run.

CARRIE Put your clothes on first. You've got a long way to go in your underwear.

LILY (*Stares down at her nightgown*) Please you go, Miss Carrie.

CARRIE Oh, I don't think so

LILY Say I'm not angry, not anything like that. Say I know what it is to love and if at the end of a year, she wants and Julian wants— Well, then. Then.

CARRIE I don't think I could say those things.

LILY You don't talk the way you did. You talk real mean.

CARRIE In the last day I lost my brother, my sister, my job. That's all I had to lose. Perhaps it's the fear of losing people that makes us talk nice or better. (*Very loudly, sharply*) Don't you think? Don't you think maybe?

LILY Do I talk different?

CARRIE You are still the baby-rich girl, teething on other people. In a few years I think you'll have to start doing something for yourself.

LILY A few years? A few days will be too late, a few minutes— What time is it? What time is Julian going to take her away?

CARRIE (*Carefully*) I did not say he was going to take her away. He has gone to meet Mrs. Warkins, evidently to give her a share.

LILY What time is it? I know Mr. Cyrus Warkins, he's Mama's lawyer. Mrs. Warkins is a sad lady, if she's the one who was on the train.

CARRIE She's ailing, I've always heard, and doesn't go into society. But I suppose the real reason is that she's part nigger and thought somebody would find out. Julian didn't mind. Imagine that. He didn't mind.

LILY Why should he? I don't mind Henry's being colored. I like negro people, and Jewish, and once I met two Irish ladies. I just hate Henry because he's Henry.

(*There is a long pause; as if* LILY *has dozed*)

CARRIE (*Watching* LILY, *sighs*) Your mind wanders, doesn't it? Go pack your bags now.

LILY You're a fine lady. He'd listen to you. Miss Carrie, please call Mr. Cyrus Warkins.

CARRIE I will not call Mr. Cyrus Warkins. His wife is not going to New York with me.

LILY Mama should call him. Where's Mama? She went for my ring. Will Mr. Warkins listen to me. Nobody does. (*She runs to pick up the phone book, opens it, and drops the book*) Don't you want to help me? It's hot.

CARRIE Wait for your Mama.

LILY It will be too late.

CARRIE I think so.

LILY You're teasing me. It's not nice to tease me and to pretend that you're not (*As* CARRIE *moves away*) Miss Carrie, please.

CARRIE (*Sharply*) What do you want of me? What is that you want?

LILY I don't want to be in the room alone. (*Points down to the telephone*) It's for the best, the best for everybody, isn't it?

CARRIE What's the sense of answering you? You just go on talking and talking.

LILY No, please. Please. Isn't it best for everybody?

CARRIE I don't know about everybody. I'm not used to thinking that way. I just think about what's best for us, for Julian.

LILY That's what I want, too. What's best for Julian. Please tell me.

CARRIE (*Carefully, as if anxious to impress the words*) I don't know that I can. The people in the bank always talk of Mr. Warkins as a low-high-born man, tough and tricky, with plenty of riffraff friends to do his dirty work. Julian isn't fit to deal with such a man and God knows what could happen. Warkins is not a man to joke with.

LILY (*After the words "what could happen,"* LILY *has picked up the phone and given the operator the number "LaFitte 1707." Her voice is firm*) Tell Mr. Warkins that Lily Berniers, Lily Prine, must speak to him immediately and does not wish to be kept waiting. (*Waiting, she smiles at* CARRIE) I think that's the way Mama would say it. Oh, hello, Mr. Cyrus, this is Lily. (*She puts the phone down, wipes her hand on her nightgown, picks up the phone, waits*) Mr. Cyrus, you mustn't blame anybody if I tell you something. Will you promise a sacred promise on the life of your child?

CARRIE He hasn't got a child.

LILY But you haven't got a child. (*Pause*) Then why did you make a sacred promise on a child you haven't got? You mustn't joke with me, Mr. Cyrus, you must not. Oh. I see. Well, please tell your wife I'm not mad a bit. That's first. Just ask her to give me one more year with Julian and then I'll promise— Well, that's all. Just ask her that. (*She listens*) I wouldn't like to say because I don't understand much myself. Why does it matter? I don't see why it should. Oh. Well, Miss Carrie heard—(CARRIE *wheels about*) A *lady* heard Henry say it. Henry? Why, the Henry of my mother—you know. Just that once, a long time ago, Julian had been kind to your wife, and that maybe she was helping him now. I don't know how Henry knew. (*After a second*) Oh, yes. I do. Henry is cousin to Mrs. Warkins. Yes, cousin. (*She waits, looks puzzled*) Mr. Cyrus? Mr. Cyrus? No, I don't think your wife's coming here. If she were, I could have asked her myself. I thought you could go right away, before she gets on the train—(*To* CARRIE) He wants to know where he can find her to give her my message. (*Into phone*) I don't know.

Rochelle Oliver and Maureen Stapleton,
as LILY and CARRIE BERNIERS

CARRIE Something about Sailor's Lane near the depot.

LILY Something about Sailor's Lane near the depot. Yes. Nobody's done anything bad, you understand, Mr. Cyrus, and tell her I know that, but I'd just like to ask to have Julian for one more— Mr. Cyrus? Well, thank you. (*She puts the phone down, sits, smiles*) He says he sure will go talk to her.

(CARRIE *sighs, waits, and then turns away.* ANNA *comes into the room, dressed in a suit. She looks at* LILY, *who does not notice her. She crosses to the table and picks up the envelope with the boat tickets*)

ANNA We can't go together now. What would you like to do about these boat tickets?

CARRIE We can't go together *now?* I don't know what you mean. Were we ever going?

ANNA I thought so. When Julian brought these home to us, he thought so.

CARRIE How strange you are. Did Julian think that? I suppose so; one piece of nonsense makes for ten. We never in our lives had any intention of going, you know that as well as I do.

(ANNA *picks up the valise, takes it to the porch and exits*)

LILY I did right, just exactly. Didn't I? And I'll take the knife of truth and swear to keep my word—

CARRIE Yes. But would you do it someplace else? It would be nice to see you in a dress. Why don't you try it?

LILY Oh. All right.

(*She exits.* CARRIE *sits down, as if exhausted. She looks at her watch.* ANNA *comes back into the room, wearing a hat now, and carrying a coat*)

ANNA You never wanted to go to Europe? Never meant to go?

CARRIE How do you know such things? You go on talking the way you always talked, saying you like or want what you always said. (ANNA *doesn't answer.* CARRIE *begins to recite in a make-fun singsong*)

"On the fairest time of June
You may go, with sun or moon
Or the seven stars to light you
Or the polar ray to right you,"—

Do you still like it, all the nights you read it to us?

ANNA Yes. (*Slowly*) I don't know. I suppose it doesn't mean much to me any more.

CARRIE I can hear you, all your cultured evenings.
(*Recites*)

"To see the laurel wreath on high suspended,
That is to crown our name when life is ended."

ANNA (*Standing near the piano, she plays*) And you this? So deeply felt, your favorite.

CARRIE Was it?

ANNA (*Smiles*) And the candied oranges I brought each week?

CARRIE I was sick of them ten years ago.

ANNA (*Softly*) Well, people change and forget to tell each other. Too bad—causes so many mistakes. (*She crosses to the table, takes a ship's ticket from the envelope, puts the envelope back on the table*) I've taken my ticket, left yours in the envelope. You'll explain about that to Julian.

CARRIE What are you talking about?

ANNA I'll spend the night at the hotel. I'm going to Europe tomorrow.

CARRIE (*Moves toward her, stares at her, starts to laugh*) You will be lonely.

ANNA That's all right. I always have been.

CARRIE You will look very silly, a middle-aged, scared-to-death woman, all by herself, trying to have a good time.

ANNA You will stay here until you sell the house?

CARRIE I don't believe you mean to go anywhere. It's just too crazy. You've never been anyplace in your life.

ANNA (*Moves toward the door*) We have said good-bye.

CARRIE You're showing off. You're just plain showing off. You're not going anywhere—(*As* ANNA *reaches the door*) You can't go before Julian. It would kill him to know that anything was wrong between us.

ANNA You don't love me, but you want me to stay with you.

CARRIE We will find a way to live.

ANNA No.

CARRIE You need me. You always have. Julian, everybody, always thought you the strong and sturdy—

ANNA And you the frail, the flutterer, the small. That's the way you wanted them to think. I knew better. Our patched-together supper, a little talk, sometimes a book, long ago on the piano, a game of casino, your bath, then mine, your room and my room, two doors closed.

CARRIE All those years of nights, all the things you knew and never said. Does everybody live like that, or just two old maids?

ANNA I loved you and so whatever I knew didn't matter. You wanted to see yourself a way you never were. Maybe that's a game you let people play when you love them. Well, we had made something together, and the words would have stayed where they belonged as we waited for our brother to need us again. But our brother doesn't need us any more, and so the poor house came down.

CARRIE I think our brother will need us. Now or someday. And we must stay together for it. (*Softly*) You're the kind of woman with no place to go, no place to go. (*Smiles*) You see? Some of those nights I thought about you, too. We must find a way to live.

ANNA I don't wish to find a way to live without you. I am a woman who has no place to go, but I am going, and after a while I will ask myself why I took my mother's two children to be my own.

CARRIE Go unpack your bags.

ANNA (*With great force*) Pretend it's last week. You've just told the girls in the bank that you can't have coffee, you have to hurry home, that Anna will be mad at you for being late, that Anna gives the orders to the soft and tender you. Go back and pretend it's still last week. (*She moves out to the porch, picks up a camellia plant and carries it down the steps.* MRS. PRINE *appears.* HENRY *is with her, he waits beyond the garden fence*) Will I look very foolish carrying a camellia plant to Europe?

ALBERTINE I don't think so. It's most becoming. Soft around the face.

(LILY *appears. She is dressed, has on her hat, and is neat and cheerful*)

LILY (*To* ANNA) Are you coming to New York with us? I would like that, Miss Anna.

ANNA You shouldn't like it, and I'm not coming with you. (*She moves around the side of the house*) I guess two plants ain't more foolish than one.

LILY Good-bye, Mama. We're going away. Good-bye. (*Smiles*) I know that will make you happy.

ALBERTINE Here's your ring, Lily.

LILY Oh. Thank you. I had forgotten— Oh. Madame Celeste gave it to you?

ALBERTINE Madame Celeste sold it to me.

LILY That's not fair, is it? Now I must give her back the knife of truth. (*She turns as if to leave*) I'd like to keep it, but she'd never sell it.

ALBERTINE (*Very sharply*) Sit down. (LILY *sits down;* ALBERTINE *sits opposite her, and speaks very quietly, but as if the words had been rehearsed*) I've had enough of whatever you're doing. However innocent is your innocence, I've had enough. More important, it is leading you into dangerous alleys. Not even for you will I again spend time in what you call an upstairs room with a morphine addict who holds séances to cover up what she sells.

LILY (*In a fury*) I don't believe you, I don't believe you, I don't believe you. You want to take my friend from me—

ALBERTINE I am tired. I am sad. It is not good to know that my child swore fidelity to such a woman, and gave her wedding ring as proof.

LILY My friend is a sweet friend. I gave her my ring because she loved me and gave me courage—

ALBERTINE You are a pure girl and I believe you. Now listen: I am going to give you a good-bye present. Try to make use of it: the pure and the innocent sometimes bring harm to themselves and those they love and, when they do, for some reason that I do not know, the injury is very great.

LILY (*Who hasn't heard a word*) You have talked this way about my friend because you want to bring me pain. Henry makes plans to pain me—(*Outside the fence,* HENRY *turns*) As you lie in bed with him, Henry makes the plans and tells you what to do.

ALBERTINE (*Pleasantly, turns toward* HENRY) Is that what we do in bed? (*To* LILY) You think that's what we do in bed? You're wrong. It's where I forget the mistakes I made with you.

HENRY Stop it.

ALBERTINE (*Ignores him; as if she is out of his control*) If something is the matter with you, come home and I will care for you, as I should, as I should. But if nothing is the matter with you, have pity and leave me alone. I tried with you all your life, but I did not do well, and for that I ask your pardon. But don't punish me forever, Lily.

LILY (*Softly*) Is something the matter with me, Mama?

(HENRY *moves toward* ALBERTINE *and holds up his hand.* ALBERTINE *stares at him, then nods*)

ALBERTINE (*Very gently*) No, darling. Certainly not.

LILY If Julian leaves me—

ALBERTINE Julian loves you, Lily.

LILY I have sent a message and will keep my word. If Mrs. Warkins will give me one year—

ALBERTINE (*After a second*) You sent a message to Mrs. Warkins? Why?

LILY Oh, because. I spoke to Mr. Warkins and told him to ask her to wait for Julian for one more year. (ALBERTINE *moves forward.* HENRY *moves toward her.* ALBERTINE *turns and stares at* HENRY) After that, if Julian doesn't want me— Where would I ever go, who would ever want me? I'm trouble, we all know that. I wouldn't have anywhere to go.

ALBERTINE (*After a long pause*) You will come home to me. You are my child.

LILY (*Warmly, sweetly*) Thank you, Mama. Nice of you. But I couldn't go home to you any more, as long as—

HENRY If it ever happens, I won't be there. I won't be there.

LILY Oh, thank you, Henry. That will be fine.

(*On the first part of* LILY'S *speech,* HENRY *sees* JULIAN *in the street.* HENRY *makes a sudden move toward him, stops.* JULIAN *appears, stumbling toward the house. His face and hands are cut and bruised. He has been beaten, and one leg is injured. He moves toward the garden in great pain; his face is so stern that the people who see him know that to assist him would be to undignify him.* ANNA, *who has seen him from the back of the house, starts toward him, then moves swiftly back as if on an errand.* LILY *does not move, but makes a loud sound.* JULIAN *tries to go up the steps of the porch, slips, and then clings to pillar of the porch.* CARRIE *moves toward him, and then backs into the room.* HENRY *goes toward* JULIAN, *but* JULIAN *puts up a hand, and* HENRY *halts*)

JULIAN I took Charlotte to her brother's house. She'll be all right, but not her face. She's safe there, I think— Do you know what Charlotte I'm talking about?

HENRY Yes.

JULIAN She'd better not stay where she is. Just in case. Not in this town.

HENRY All right.

(*Painfully, slowly,* JULIAN *moves into the room.* CARRIE, *standing near the phone, points toward it*)

CARRIE (*Softly*) Doctor?

JULIAN No. (ANNA *comes in carrying a basin and bandages*) My friend. My poor friend. All she wanted, saved for, thought about—(*He gasps as if he is sick*)—to get away forever. Standing there, standing in the alley, they slashed us up.

ALBERTINE (*Who is standing on the porch; softly*) Who?

JULIAN I don't know who. I saw two men and then I didn't see anything else. Two thugs he sent—

ALBERTINE Who sent?

JULIAN (*In a shout*) Mr. Cyrus Warkins sent his men to meet us. (*He takes the money envelope from his coat pocket where it has been arranged as if it were a handkerchief, crumbles it, and throws it to the ground*) Nobody knew she came to Chicago to tell me, nobody knew she put up the money for the land, nobody knew her name. Tell her I swear it, I swear it. (*To* ANNA, *who comes toward him with bandages*) Go away. (*To* HENRY) I told *nobody*. Tell her I swear it on my life—

HENRY No need to tell her that.

JULIAN *But somebody did know. Somebody told him.* My friend—wanted to help me, took a dangerous chance and did—(*Softly*) You should see her. You should see her. Make her know I never spoke her name.

ALBERTINE She will not think you did. I am certain she will not think you did.

JULIAN (*Points to the envelope*) That's what's left of the money.

ALBERTINE Shall I go to the police for you, Julian?

JULIAN I went. High up, to Drummond.

ALBERTINE Then perhaps—

JULIAN No. I don't know what the thugs looked like— No matter what I said I could see Drummond saying to himself that I made it up, never could have had fifty dollars in my pocket, not less a hundred fifty thousand—

ALBERTINE Shall I go to Warkins?

JULIAN What for? Is he going to tell you who told him, who he hired to beat us up— What for?

ALBERTINE I don't know.

JULIAN Christ, what a mess-ass I am. She handed me the whole deal, told me every move to make, a baby could have done it. *(His leg collapses and he falls to the floor. Slowly, painfully he lifts himself, moves toward the chair and table.* ALBERTINE *turns away, as if the sight is painful. As* JULIAN *falls to the floor,* LILY *makes a dash to the porch.* ALBERTINE *moves toward her; puts out a hand to hold her)*

LILY Mama, I did it.

ALBERTINE Are you very sure you love him?

LILY Mama, I did it. God forgive me.

ALBERTINE Go in and sit by him. Just sit by him and shut up. Can you do that? Can you have enough pity for him not to kill him with the truth? Can you love him enough to go by him, sit down—*(Very softly, with great violence)*—*and be still?* (LILY *nods)* Then go and do it.

(LILY *moves into the house and timidly approaches* JULIAN)

JULIAN I don't look nice. Take off your hat, baby. We ain't going nowhere. There ain't nothing to go with.

LILY May I wash your face?

JULIAN Don't look like that. I'm all right. Nobody ever beat me up before, or slashed a friend.

CARRIE Things can happen.

JULIAN What did you say?

CARRIE I said bad things happen to people. Doesn't mean anything.

JULIAN I mean the way you said it. Say it that way again.

CARRIE I don't know what you mean. Why don't you go rest yourself, darling. Good hot bath—

JULIAN (*Turns to stare at her*) Why you start to purr at me? As if I'd done something good—(*Moves toward her*) You're smiling. What the hell's there to smile at? You *like* me this way? (*After a second, turns to stare at the room*) Pretty, all this. And the mortgage, and the tickets to Europe, and all the fun to come. Pretty, wasn't it?

CARRIE We didn't want them. (*To* ANNA) Did we?

ANNA No, we didn't want them.

JULIAN Don't talk that way. Won't do me any good. Assing it up all my God damned life, all my life it's been the same. (*With violence*) Nobody ever beat me up before. Nobody's ever going to beat me up again.

(*There is a pause.* LILY, *who has been washing* JULIAN's *face, turns away.* CARRIE *sighs and moves to the porch door. Then, as if a decision has been made, she moves out to the porch and leans down to pick up* ANNA's *luggage*)

ALBERTINE (*Very sharply, to* CARRIE) Mean to see a man stoke his pride. The meanest sight in the world. Don't you think?

CARRIE Let's be glad nothing worse happened. We're together, the three of us, that's all that matters.

ALBERTINE I counted four.

CARRIE I mean the four of us.

ALBERTINE Someday you will tell him about Lily? Then there will be three of you. Before you tell him, let me know. I will want to come for her.

CARRIE (*Points inside*) All that stuff has to go back, and the debts, got to find ourselves jobs. So much to do.

(CARRIE *picks up the valises and moves into the room*)

JULIAN Old saying, money is a real pure lady and when the world began she swore herself an oath never to belong to a man who didn't love her. I never loved her and she guessed it. Couldn't fool her, she got good sense. (*Softly, desperately*) Nobody ever beat me up before. Maybe once it starts—

CARRIE There's bad luck and there's good luck. That's all.

JULIAN I guess so. Well, I've had the bad. Maybe I got a little good luck coming to me. Other men make it easy. Plenty of room in this world for everybody. Just got to fight for it. Got to start again, start again.

(*He rises.* LILY *moves to help him*)

CARRIE I'm going to get something nice to make soup with. You always liked a good soup when you didn't feel well. Meat and marrow, the way you like it. (*As she gets to the porch door*) Tomorrow's another day. (JULIAN, *leaning on* LILY, *moves out.* CARRIE, *leaving the house, passes* HENRY *and* ALBERTINE *in the garden*) Good-bye, Mrs. Prine.

(*She exits. After a second* HENRY *puts his hand on* ALBERTINE'S *shoulder*)

HENRY Good-bye.

(HENRY *exits.* ANNA *crosses to pick up her large valise, and at the same time* ALBERTINE *rises to exit*)

*Curtain*